An Intentionally Specific 3-St. [...] [...]

For Guy

Embrace
the A·R·T
of Forgiveness
& Repentance

(A)ctivation

(R)estoration

(T)ransformation

God Bless You each time you embrace

p. 124

Rose Carlin

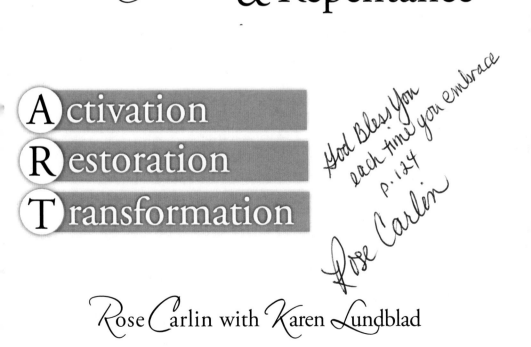

Rose Carlin with Karen Lundblad

© Copyright 2015 Rose Carlin with Karen Lundblad. All Rights Reserved

Printed in the USA

ISBN (print): 978-0-9969364-0-8
ISBN (Kindle): 978-0-9969364-1-5
ISBN (eBook): 978-0-9969364-2-2
Library of Congress Control Number (LCCN): 2015955500

To contact the authors:
www.embracetheART.org

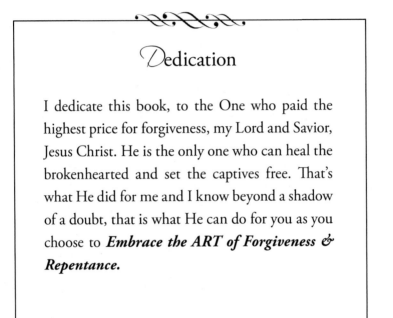

Dedication

I dedicate this book, to the One who paid the highest price for forgiveness, my Lord and Savior, Jesus Christ. He is the only one who can heal the brokenhearted and set the captives free. That's what He did for me and I know beyond a shadow of a doubt, that is what He can do for you as you choose to **Embrace the ART of Forgiveness & Repentance.**

Praise for *Embrace The A.R.T. of Forgiveness & Repentance*

Rose Carlin and Karen Lundblad have co-authored a remarkable and practical "tool" to help a Christian experience genuine forgiveness and repentance. Their explanation unravels what for many are misunderstood concepts, even for long-time Christians. I am thrilled with the clarity at which they exegete each theological concept and the practicality by which they lead the reader into "the heaven of forgiveness." To be set free from bitterness and resentment is a gift of incalculable value. Such a gift is available to those who will read this book and put to work it's teaching.

Dr. John Guest
Author
Founding Pastor, Christ Church at Grove Farm, Pittsburgh, PA
Co-founder, Trinity School of Ministry, Ambridge, PA
Founder, Coalition for Christian Outreach, Nationwide

What you hold in your hand, *Embrace The A.R.T. of Forgiveness & Repentance*, will transform and restore your hope, joy, and purpose.

Sheila M. Stephens, Pharm.D.
President, Stephens Compounding Pharmacy
Hilton Head, South Carolina
Duke Certified Integrative Health Coach

I have been around ministry for 34 years and I believe the reason many people never achieve God's best for their life is because they have allowed a root of bitterness to poison them from the inside out. This book will help every believer gain victory over the enemy through the intentionally specific 3-step prayer model. I pray you will apply these principles and embrace the life God has for you.

Dr. Ronnie Phillips, Jr.
Senior Associate Pastor, Abba's House
Hixson, Tennessee

When I get tired or discouraged all it takes to get me going again is to read a book like this one. Rose's testimony in chapter one will inspire you to believe that God really cares and has answers for your challenges. She will inspire you to actually do what the scriptures teach and then you will have the same results she has.

Rose and Karen have taken proven scriptural principles and explained them in their own words and personality. Their teaching and these principles will enrich your life and greatly bless you ... only IF you actually apply the principles to your life. This is why they so carefully explain them in a way that we can all understand. This book will motivate you to actually follow the instruction of our Messiah, Jesus when He says, "If you love me obey me."

Dr. Art Mathias
Founder, Wellspring School of Ministry
Anchorage, Alaska

I am elated to endorse *Embrace the A.R.T. of Forgiveness & Repentance* because I feel responsible for setting it's existence into motion. I invited Rose to attend the Forgiveness Conference eight years ago, changing the course of her destiny. Rose has shared her divine discovery of freedom with astounding clarity as she and Karen guide you on a step-by-step forgiveness journey with the precision of a finely tuned navigational system.

Captain Denise Blankinship
Commercial Airline Pilot
Honoree on the Wall of Honor at the Smithsonian
National Air and Space Museum
First Father/Daughter Airline Captains in the World (1982)

Embrace the A.R.T. of Forgiveness & Repentance is a must read! It contains vital information that people need to discover and implement in their daily lives and relationships. One thing is certain, at some point, someone is going to hurt or offend you. This book teaches you how to extinguish that offense, to take back control of your emotions and forgive those who have hurt or offended you. As a CEO I personally have to put these steps into practice in my business as I deal with employees and customers. I can only image how much better the world would be if this vital information was put into practice.

David Rusk
CEO Integrity Electrical Contractors, Inc.
Las Vegas, Nevada

This is not a read-only book. The pages hold a treasure map containing simple, yet profound truths. When following these action steps of truth it will lead you to the treasure—freedom. We know from personal experience this journey will take you from bondage to freedom, from depression to overwhelming joy, from hopelessness and despair to abundant living. As the title denotes, Rose and Karen have created a masterpiece in *Embrace the A.R.T. of Forgiveness & Repentance.* They clearly show us, there really is an art to forgiving.

Donna and Ronny Barron
Pastors and Founders of China Hill International Ministries
Rhine, Georgia

There was a season in my life where I was just trying to keep my head above water as I was going through a divorce and building my own business. That was years ago and now my life is in order, business is strong, a ministry was birthed, and my family is healthy. Rose taught me many spiritual principles, which are contained in this book, but first and foremost was how to forgive. Like me, I know you will be empowered through this teaching and experience healing in your life.

Amanda May
Beauty Evangelist
Creator of DIVINE Image Cosmetics
Founder of I AM Worthy Foundation
Author of *Unlock, Keys To Beauty From Within*

I used the truths in this book to take me, step-by-step, out of my old wounds and hurts into a new, firm foundation of healing and restoration. Receive the truths in this book. They will help you become an overcomer, so you can take back your life and fulfill your destiny.

Deborah Rush
Jesus Follower
Wife, Mother, and Grandmother

I first met Rose Carlin in 2005 on a tour to Israel where we were roommates. I began to see that hiding behind the vivacious personality was a woman who was not well—physically or emotionally. Two years later we attended the Wellspring School of Ministry together. That is when her journey of healing began. I can verify that the Rose writing this book in 2015 is not the same Rose I met ten years ago. I have watched the progression of her life as she has passionately given her all to "walk the talk" of love and forgiveness. The radical changes in her are proof that by inviting God into the forgiveness equation and using the power of Jesus' name and His shed blood, a completely changed life is possible. If you are ready to stop an unhealthy cycle that unforgiveness brings, then follow the plan laid out in this book. Don't wait to forgive. It isn't easy, but it's worth it.

Durlene Williams
Certified Wellspring Prayer Minister

$\mathscr{A}$cknowledgement

When creating this easy-to-remember acronym (A.R.T.), what I did not foresee was the three letters I chose would spell a word, let alone the first name of the man who introduced me to these principles from his book, *Biblical Foundations of Freedom*. I could hardly wait to tell Dr. Art Mathias that my book would be named for and dedicated to him. I will never forget the day he humbly declined to receive accolades, but encouraged me to give credit where credit is due. "Yes sir," I responded, so here it is.

With great admiration and deepest thanks for his life saving ministry, I take this opportunity to credit the teachings and ministry of Dr. Art Mathias, founder of Wellspring Ministries of Alaska as the motivation and source of information contained in these pages. His additional books, *In His Own Image* and *The Continuing Works of Christ* have deepened my understanding of forgiveness.

His amazing personal testimony of physical healing through the power of forgiveness, not only propelled him into ministry but did the same for me. Once you experience the healing power of God through forgiveness and repentance, your desire is for everyone to have the same experience. Thank you, Art, for being a vessel for noble purposes.

"To forgive is to set a prisoner free and discover that the prisoner was you."

—Lewis B. Smedes

Contents

Foreword

Embrace the A.R.T. of Forgiveness & Repentance is gripping, compelling, riveting, transformational, and life-changing. Words can barely scratch the depth and significance of this book. As a result, I re-examined the way I pray, the love I demonstrate, the God I worship, and the faith I stand on.

Embrace the A.R.T. of Forgiveness & Repentance is unlike any other book you've ever read or will ever read. It will eradicate limitations, barriers, and strongholds which have held you back from pursuing your God-given destiny.

It will dislodge destructive thought patterns and rekindle a love for others and most of all for God. It will liberate you in ways you never dreamed possible.

It will take courage to brave the truths you encounter within these pages because you may see yourself in nearly every chapter of this book. That's okay. Author Rose Carlin has been shockingly honest and transparent about her own struggles, and if those struggles capture your heart, grab your attention, and initiate the healing process, they have served a divine purpose.

1

It's a book that can be read and reread, a book that pastors should distribute to parishioners. Churches should use it for group Bible studies. Couples should use it to repair marriages. Families should give it to estranged loved ones. Doctors should prescribe it to patients.

This book not only contains revelation, it possesses the seeds of revolution that will, at long last, overthrow unforgiveness, bitterness, resentment, and every other destructive mindset that has kept you shackled for far too long.

This book is an odyssey of freedom and deliverance. It's a journey you will never regret.

Mitch Fox
Broadcaster, Television Host, Anchor
Emmy-Nominated P.B.S. Producer
Director of Communications for the City of North Las Vegas

Chapter One

Before & After
A Life-Changing Transformation

Welcome to *The A.R.T. of Forgiveness & Repentance.* This is the story of an intentionally specific 3-step prayer model that has brought life-changing transformation to thousands of people—thank God, I am one of them. This A.R.T. prayer model is the tool I used to navigate the highway to freedom from bitterness and to find healing from the residual pain left by life's disappointments and traumas. This A.R.T. prayer literally **rocked** my world, **saved** my marriage, **healed** my body, **removed** my mask, and totally **changed** my career.

I was introduced to this "better way to pray" at a forgiveness conference taught by Dr. Art Mathias eight years ago. He skillfully wove three biblical truths into forgiveness prayers, and I needed a way to remember them. I decided to create an acronym that would help me recall these truths in my prayer time, so that I wouldn't be dependent upon the notes I took from his teachings. This prayer was so powerful that I wanted to apply it daily in my life and have a simple way to teach it to others. I decided to identify each step with it's own capital letter that reflected it's unique purpose. This is how the 3-step prayer model, *The A.R.T. of Forgiveness & Repentance* was born.

A—Step One

I was taught to **ACTIVATE** my <u>A</u>uthority over the enemy of my soul (the devil), who is actively seeking to destroy my ability to live an abundant life and fulfill my God-given destiny. I discovered that every time I got disappointed or offended by someone, an unseen enemy showed up full of *accusations* and *judgment* designed to plant a root of bitterness in me. Those bad *"works"* of the enemy had to be removed from my life and this step of the prayer did just that!

R—Step Two

I was taught to **R**equest and **R**eceive the Holy Spirit of God to **RESTORE** my broken heart and relationships. This step invites God to replace the space that the enemy strongman held with the STRONGERMAN instead—the Holy Spirit!

T—Step Three

I was taught to <u>T</u>ake <u>T</u>ime at the end of the prayer and ask for God to <u>T</u>ell me His <u>T</u>ruth. Then I learned to make a very healthy choice and transplant God's truth over the lies from the enemy in my mind. This is a crucial step towards **TRANSFORMATION**.

You can see how labeling and identifying the 3 steps became easy to remember through alliterations since there were so many intentions and actions that started with the very same letter!

What You Can Expect

In this book, you will be given the steps for how to embrace this A.R.T. You will find them clearly presented in a practical application format, like a "manual" explaining how to use a tool. Detailed explanations and the supporting scriptures are included along with prayer "scripts" for you to use. Why? Because knowledge without application is like a car without fuel. A car is nice to have, but without fuel, it gets you absolutely nowhere. The goal of this book is to not only encourage you to begin moving down the highway toward your personal freedom, but also to empower you by providing the essentials for a successful journey. Along the way you will notice, my GPS action steps for you are marked **CHOOSE2.** Like a billboard advertises to a driver, these **CHOOSE2** signs are meant to grab your attention and encourage you to take action. Your destination of freedom depends on it.

Every story of transformation has a "before" and an "after." I humbly submit my story to you now. Like everyone who had an encounter with Jesus never came away the same, I am not the same person I was just eight years ago. The dramatic before and after condition of the interior lining of my esophagus, stomach, and colon—documented in my medical chart—is a testimony to the healing power of God and just one of the five ways I've been personally transformed.

This is My Story

My name is Rose and my best friend is Karen. Together we are going to tell you my story of physical and spiritual transformation … once I discovered that I had a lot to learn about forgiveness. To be honest, this was surprising for me because I literally thought that I had already forgiven everyone. Not only that, I had been raised in the church all my life so I knew that I "had-to." What I know <u>now</u> is "how–to."

The reason I have a story of transformation to share today is because I decided to "**CHOOSE2.**"

On my quest to understand more about forgiveness, it became apparent to me that my version of forgiving others was actually done more out of obligation than anything else.

It was just something I felt was expected of me.

As a child, I would hear, "Say you are sorry to your sister," and obediently I would. Then I would hear mom coach my sister to say, "Now, tell Rose that she is forgiven. You two make up!" Throughout my formative years, this pattern replayed back and forth, like a game of ping-pong. This verbal exchange became embedded as my auto-response each time someone told me that they were sorry. This unchallenged thinking did not serve me well, especially as an adult, and particularly not with my mother.

A mother who becomes your "best friend" in your teenage years, living her life through yours doesn't fare so well when you leave her behind for college, then get married and move to the other side of the country. Unknown to me, in my absence my mom got a "new" best friend … Jack Daniels. I never saw that coming! Our family never had alcohol in the house. NEVER.

Six years later, at the age of 27, I was invited back home for a surprise baby shower for one of my best friends from high school. What I didn't know was that the shower was planned as a surprise for me as well. I was five months pregnant. My old gang had been secretly planning this party with my mom. The biggest surprise of the day, however, came as mom arrived an hour late, stumbling through the door, singing "Happy Birthday," and tripping over herself, knocking the beautiful cake decorated with blue icing celebrating the baby boy I was carrying, to the floor.

My memories of that day were of me on my hands and knees trying to scrub the blue icing out of my friend's pure white carpet and the smell of my mom's breath as she came rushing to my side and repeatedly said, "I'm sorry ... I'm sorry, Rose. Please forgive me, please forgive me." That was the day, for the first time in my life, I chose ***"not-to."***

I was devastated, hurt, embarrassed, disappointed, offended, repulsed, angry, and mad. As I let the "sun go down on my anger" night after night, it festered and embedded deeper and deeper into a root of bitterness. This root was nourished by a voice of self-pity inside my head that replayed continually, "How could she do that to me?" I believed I had every right to be angry and that if I forgave her, it meant I was letting her off the hook. In my mind, that wasn't fair. She didn't deserve my forgiveness. She was at fault, and needed to pay for the injustice!

> *I believed if I forgave her it meant I was letting her off the hook.*

A few weeks passed and then one night we finally had a sober phone conversation. She apologized profusely, saying that she never meant to hurt me and admitted that her drinking was out of control. She promised to get help and NEVER take a drink again. After her repeated requests for my forgiveness, I felt very sorry for her and said, "Okay mom, I forgive you." We both cried and with sincere words of love, I committed to assist her with finding professional help. As we hung up, I thought to myself, "Okay, I'm over it. I forgave her, let it go. Now it's time to move on." I compartmentalized the whole experience as just being the worst day of my life. I was wrong.

Four months later, on Christmas Day 1985, I called mom to let her know that her first grandson was delivered at 5:30, but there was nothing to celebrate. He was not breathing. My baby was born dead. That Christmas was the single most Silent Night of my life because Christopher Robert Carlin was, and still is, sleeping in heavenly peace.

There are no words that adequately express my inconsolable sorrow from my loss, but there are words that describe my reaction to having empty arms. I got mad. This time, however, there was no one to blame, no one at fault, no one to pay for the injustice. My doctor had performed flawlessly. A thorough inspection of the baby revealed nothing physically wrong, the umbilical cord was not wrapped around his neck, I had taken every vitamin, followed every prenatal instruction, and attended every doctor's appointment. So, where do you put your anger when it has nowhere to go? Mine went inward and upward. I got mad at myself and I also got mad at God. This was not done consciously. In fact, I had no knowledge that I did, until 23 years later when I attended the forgiveness conference. This is what I now know for sure … anger buried alive, NEVER dies, even as the years pass by.

My "Before" Picture

I never lost the weight I gained from pregnancy. In fact, I started to gain more as food became a source of comfort and entertainment. Five years later after a second pregnancy and second loss, thanks be to God, I delivered a perfectly healthy baby girl. She was and still is today the unquestionable apple of my eye. Even with newfound happiness and contentment, I struggled to lose that baby weight as well. Each attempt to cut out carbs and calories ended in failure and embedded a faulty belief that "I can't control this area of my life." Food had a hold on me, and like mom, it had graduated to an addiction.

Along with obesity, I had over 200 red and irritated ulcerations on the lining of my stomach and colon, plus five other clinically diagnosed diseases for which I was taking prescription medication. My marriage was in shambles and my husband and I were separated with plans for divorce.

One day at an emergency appointment for excruciating stomach pain, my doctor told me that I was headed down the road to an early grave because the ulcers in my stomach were now bleeding.

After hearing his assessment of my future, I was reminded of the words I read a few months earlier, the night I walked mom home to heaven from her room in the Alzheimers Unit. There were three words written on her Death Certificate as the cause of death: "Failure to Thrive." I knew in my heart as I reflected on them, they not only described her life as an alcoholic and as an Alzheimer's victim, but they aptly described my life as well. This was my wake up call. I had to find an exit ramp off this road to an early grave.

My "After" Picture

As I sit typing this book, I am 58 years old, weighing 100 pounds less, still married to my husband of 37 years, disease and symptom free and taking NO medications ... not even antacids. At my last visit to the same doctor, after reviewing the photographs of the endoscopy and colonoscopy with me that showed healthy, pink tissue, free of lesions, he wrote the word "stunned" on my medical chart. I am pretty sure that is a word he did not learn in medical school.

Now you can understand why I began this chapter with raving reviews about this prayer model. It did indeed:

- **Rock my world** by introducing me to biblical truths I had not been taught in church. I was perishing without this information. First and foremost I learned that I am a target of an <u>active</u> enemy on assignment to destroy me with his "works" and unforgiveness was one of them! Also, that each disappointment, hurt and offense (whether large or small), created an opportunity for the enemy to wage a demonic assault on my thinking, causing me to accuse God, others, and myself. Then the light bulb moment ... I needed God's power to help me forgive instead of trying to forgive on my own. Inviting God to be involved has had astonishing results.

- **Save my marriage** by teaching me that my battle was NOT against flesh and blood (a.k.a. my husband). The prayer scripts became the actual tool we both needed to have ready at a moment's notice, to use against our real enemy! Some days, the tool was used a lot! We just celebrated our thirty-seventh anniversary and he often reminds me that if it weren't for him,

I wouldn't have had so many opportunities to practice the prayer!

- **Heal my body** from the following diagnosis: clinical depression (medicated for 20 years), ulcerative colitis, bleeding stomach ulcers, IBD/food allergies, severe esophageal acid reflux and damage, sleep apnea, and obesity. The medications included: anti-depressants, anti-anxiety, anti- spasmodic, anti-acid, anti-inflammatory, and anti-histamine and one sleep apparatus.

- **Remove my mask.** For years, I wore a fake "smiley-faced" mask that I used to hide my emotional pain. I successfully performed in the roles of "people pleaser," "life of the party," and "cheerful wife and mother " who portrayed having her act together. Today, the smile on my face is genuine and the only facemask I wear is the anti-aging and hydrating type!

- **Change my career** from a public school music teacher and choir director to a Christian Life Coach, Ordained Prayer Minister and founder of Embrace the ART, a 501c3, non-profit organization established to educate, encourage, and ignite a revival of forgiveness! My daughter best describes my drastic career change when she tells her friends what I do. She says, "My mom exchanged her piano for pom-poms! She's a forgiveness cheerleader now, but her uniform isn't a cute little skirt. She wears combat boots and packs a powerful prayer to take down the enemy of unforgiveness." She's right. I do enthusiastically encourage others to embrace the desires of God's heart and make the CHOICE to forgive and repent.

God's divine plan of forgiveness and the rewards I received for repenting and being forgiven are worth shouting about! That's why both the forgiveness prayer and the repentance prayer have been intentionally linked together in this model. It's so a double burden can be released. First, by forgiving the debts of your offender, and second, by repenting and receiving forgiveness yourself for any bitterness you held as a result of being offended.

These two prayers are like a highway with two lanes heading in the same direction toward the ultimate destination … freedom. I traveled both lanes by using both prayers on my journey to physical, spiritual, and emotional healing.

My hope is that you will allow me to be your cheerleader and show you "how-to" have victory over the damaging effects caused by offenses in your life. Stay with me all the way to the end of this book as together we *Embrace the A.R.T. of Forgiveness & Repentance* … the journey from bitter to better.

Chapter Two

Forgiveness
What It Is and What It Is Not

What is forgiveness? That sounds like an easy question, but as I began my ministry providing individual prayer coaching sessions, it quickly became apparent that many people had the same misunderstandings and faulty perceptions about forgiveness that I once had. In order for their session to have the life-changing effect they desired, these had to be clarified for each person right from the start.

This book is written so that you, too, can use this tool and experience a transformed life through forgiveness. Therefore, it is important to establish a foundation of what forgiveness IS and what it IS NOT right from the beginning for you as well. A basic understanding of what forgiveness means is defined as:

Forgiveness: *the act of forgiving, pardoning a mistake or offense;* [1] *to stop being angry about, or resentful against.* [2]

I have found that a basic understanding wasn't thorough enough for most people, so I created a new definition complete with detailed instructions on "how to" achieve it. My definition is:

> **Forgiveness:** *begins with a* **CHOICE** *you make to completely* **RELEASE** *the debts of someone who hurt you from "owing" you anything,* **not even an apology,** *no matter how much they disappointed you, embarrassed you, angered you, lied to you, abandoned you, rejected you, betrayed you, or even just aggravated you. Bottom line, no matter what,* **CHOOSE2 FORGIVE**.

I realize this definition is radical, but it sets a lofty goal worth striving for. I can personally testify to huge benefits. My clients and I have experienced incredible freedom as we pressed on in prayer towards this goal.

The "how-to" is accomplished by inviting God to be involved in your choice to forgive using an intentionally specific 3-step prayer model which incorporates:

A **ACTIVATION** of your authority in the name of Jesus to destroy the works of the devil.

R Requesting and receiving **RESTORATION** for your body, mind, and soul from the Holy Spirit.

T Transplanting truth from God (into your thinking) for **TRANSFORMATION**.

Forgiveness, using the A.R.T. prayer model, has become a way of life for my clients as they practice it on a daily basis to maintain their freedom. I still practice it daily—eight years later (remember, I said I'm still married)! My prayer is that you will experience this same freedom and life-changing transformation as you continue reading. Allow me to be your personal cheerleader as I show you "how-to" ***Embrace the ART of Forgiveness & Repentance.***

> "Forgiveness is an intentional gift of kindness towards yourself; it's the gift that keeps on giving, a constant companion of the 'free indeed.'"

I hope you enjoy this collection of my favorite quotes and teachings on forgiveness as together, we establish our foundation of what forgiveness IS and IS NOT. They have been like "pearls of wisdom" to me, harvested from many teachers, preachers, books, CDs, DVDs, seminars and sermons over many years. I have strung them together for such a time as this. I owe a debt of gratitude to all of the preachers and authors, too many to individually identify, who have gone before me on this subject. I stand in agreement with them as God's cheerleader and enthusiastically announce ...

> God has a divine plan that will heal our broken hearts and set us free from the destruction of bitterness ... it's called **FORGIVENESS**.

Enjoy these "pearls" from scripture and other sources:

> "To err is human, to forgive, divine."
> —Alexander Pope

"Therefore, as the elect of God, holy and beloved, put on tender mercies, kindness, humility, meekness, long-suffering; bearing with one another, and <u>forgiving one another</u>, if anyone has a complaint against another; even as Christ forgave you, so <u>you also MUST do</u>."[3]

"Be kind and compassionate to one another, forgiving each other, just as in Christ God forgave you."[4]

Forgiveness IS: Giving a full pardon to, cancelling the debts of, wiping the slate clean from … the offenses of an offender.

Forgiveness IS NOT: Endorsing, condoning, justifying, excusing, tolerating, or approving the wrong actions of others.

Forgiveness erases their debt to YOU but does not erase their debt to GOD, *"For we must all stand before Christ to be judged."*[5]

Forgiveness IS: A virtue of the brave. Often it takes every bit of courage you have to forgive an offender.

Forgiveness IS NOT: For the coward.

Forgiveness IS: The pathway to reconciled relationships.

Forgiveness IS NOT: An obligation to reconcile a relationship with an offender. It takes one to forgive; it takes two to reconcile.

Forgiveness doesn't need to be done face-to-face; the person may even be deceased. Forgiveness can take place whether or not restoration of the relationship happens.

Forgiveness IS: ANESTHESIA for a painful memory.

Forgiveness IS NOT: AMNESIA of the memory.

Healing a memory does not remove a memory. Removing the pain radically improves the way to remember.

Forgiveness IS: A mature CHOICE, an intentional act of your free will; a decision not to keep a record of wrongs, whether the offender apologizes or admits they were wrong.

Forgiveness IS NOT: To be given out of obligation just because you were told you "had to."

Forgiveness IS: An extravagant gift from God freely given to us and is to be freely given to others, even up to 7 x 70 a day.[6]

Forgiveness IS NOT: A feeling or an emotion. Instead, it's the ultimate act of obedience. Forgive anyway, your feelings follow your choice.

Forgiveness IS: Necessary to live in peace.

Forgiveness IS NOT: Optional, especially regarding family members. Make it part of the DNA you pass on to future generations.

Forgiveness IS: A lifetime project.

Forgiveness IS NOT: A once-in-a-lifetime event.

Forgiveness IS: Possible, with God's help.

Forgiveness IS NOT: Impossible

Releasing the debts of others, including a need for an apology, is just not natural. It requires divine power to pull it off. Rest assured God would not instruct you to do something without providing the way for it to be accomplished.

> *You can do "all things through Christ*
> *who strengthens you."*[7]

The "all things" refers to the "things" God calls us to do. Forgiveness is one of them. You can do it!

Forgiveness IS: The stain remover for your past. When correctly applied, forgiveness can label your past as "over and done with." It prevents your past from showing up in your present and messing up your future.

Forgiveness IS: When you set the captive free and discover the only real prisoner was you.

Forgiveness IS: Doing What Jesus Did (DWJD). Imitating Christ allows others to see a reflection of Him in you. You resemble God when you forgive.

Forgiveness IS: A memorial to Christ's accomplished work on the cross. In the midst of the excruciating pain of crucifixion, His foremost thought and the first words out of His mouth were about forgiveness. *"Father forgive them"* . . . three simple words that sum up the reason He came to earth. God has been answering Jesus' prayer ever since it was uttered over 2,000 years ago.

My coaching sessions also revealed further misunderstandings that I call "forgiveness clichés" frequently offered as good advice but impossible to do. In fact, many people who have come to me for ministry have been wounded by these very words.

1. **FORGIVE AND FORGET**—Forgiveness is NOT forgetting. These words should not be coupled in the same sentence as if it were an option. Let's get this straight—forgetting a trauma is not possible, but removing the pain from the memory is. When the pain is removed, you can live life as if you've never been hurt.

2. **GET OVER IT ... LET IT GO ... JUST MOVE ON**—Forgiveness NEVER denies you've been HURT. You CAN'T change what happened, but you CAN change dramatically how you feel about what happened.

3. **TIME HEALS ALL WOUNDS**—Time cannot; forgiveness can. I've watched hundreds of people, myself included, be healed from mental and physical pain once they chose to *Embrace the A.R.T. of Forgiveness & Repentance.* That was something time could not do for me.

Forgiveness IS NOT: EASY—it's easier said than done.

Forgiveness IS NOT: FREE—It cost Jesus His life.

Forgiveness IS NOT: FAIR—It's a pardon for what seems to be unpardonable.

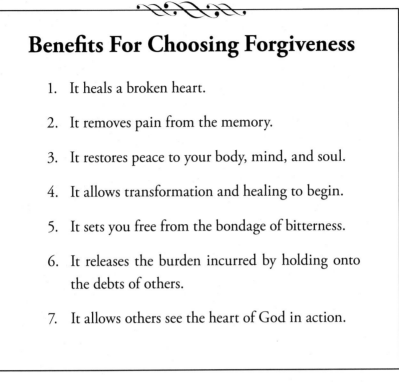

Benefits For Choosing Forgiveness

1. It heals a broken heart.

2. It removes pain from the memory.

3. It restores peace to your body, mind, and soul.

4. It allows transformation and healing to begin.

5. It sets you free from the bondage of bitterness.

6. It releases the burden incurred by holding onto the debts of others.

7. It allows others see the heart of God in action.

Liabilities For Choosing Unforgiveness

When you **CHOOSE (NOT 2)** FORGIVE, it is called unforgiveness. UNFORGIVENESS is:

1. **SIN**—Sin ruptures our relationship with God. Jesus died so we could have uninterrupted fellowship with the Father.

2. **DESTRUCTIVE**—It becomes the soil from which a root of bitterness grows. Unforgiveness spreads to every area of your life, from the root to the fruit as evidenced by the "rotten" results clearly pictured for you in chapter three.

3. **EXPENSIVE**—It will cost you more than you will ever be able to pay. It costs you your peace, your health, your joy, your relationships with God and family—all things that are priceless.

4. **HEAVY**—The debt you hold onto when you believe others "owe you" is heavy baggage. CHOOSE2 RELEASE their debt … it's the best weight loss plan of all!

5. **UNHEALTHY**—It compromises your body's state of homeostasis, robbing you of your peace. Unforgiveness cannot be hidden from God **or** from your body. It often manifests in physical infirmities.

"Bitterness is like cancer. It eats upon the host."

Maya Angelou

"Don't let unforgiveness become a memorial
to a hurt making it a concrete stumbling
block for the rest of your life."

Three Stories From "Heroes of Forgiveness"

The following is paraphrased from *The Book Of Forgiving* by Desmond Tutu, Archbishop Emeritus and Nobel Prize winner from South Africa:

"The only way to experience healing and peace is to forgive. Until we forgive we remain locked <u>into</u> our pain and locked <u>out of</u> our freedom. Without forgiveness we remain tethered to the person who harmed us. We are bound to them by chains of bitterness, tied together and trapped. Until we forgive them, they hold the keys to our happiness. They are our jailor."

From the article, "Amish Grace—How Forgiveness Transcended Tragedy:"

"The blood was barely dry on the schoolhouse floor when Amish parents brought words of forgiveness to the family of the one who had slain their daughter. Their words of forgiveness trumped the violence by arresting the world's attention for three weeks. News about the Amish forgiveness appeared in 2,900 news stories worldwide and on 534,000 websites. All religions teach forgiveness but no one does it like the Amish did that day."

From Eva Mozes Kor, Holocaust survivor from Auschwitz:

"The act of forgiveness gave me back the power that was taken away from me as a victim. As long as I held onto my anger, the ones who victimized me still had a hold on my life. You don't forgive because the perpetrator deserves it, you do it because you, the victim, deserves the right to be free once again."

From South Africa to Auschwitz with the Amish in between, you have read these words about forgiveness, validating its POWER. **No matter who you are or where you are in the world, the opportunity for you to forgive is always present and it's power is universally the same.** I have seen lives transformed right before my eyes as they have embraced this A.R.T. tool. To encourage you, some of their testimonies are included throughout the book. Their transformation stories have been my inspiration to continue my coaching ministry and to write this book. It has been the privilege of a lifetime to see marriages restored, phobias removed, the effects of post traumatic stress released, health regained, the scars of deep emotional wounds healed, addictive behaviors cease, disappointments replaced with hope, heartache replaced with joy, and conflict resolved with peace. Their stories may be different, but this one theme remains the same: there is POWER in forgiveness.

Forgiveness is a powerful tool. It changes the
memory of your past into a hope for your future.

Amish Forgiveness Makes Headlines Once Again

As this book was going into print, an article appeared in *People Magazine*, September 28, 2015. Terri Roberts, mother of Charlie Roberts, the man who shot ten Amish schoolgirls—five fatally, before taking his own life, has written her new memoir, *Forgiven*. How does one go on living when overcome with grief and shock from such a tragedy, and deal with the guilt knowing it was your son who committed such a heinous act? The title of her memoir says it all; it begins with forgiveness. When an Amish neighbor showed up at her door, hours after the shooting, to say no one blamed them or wanted them to move away, Terri said, "It felt like the grace of God walked in that door."

Forgiveness ushered in the presence of God to begin His miraculous work of piecing her life and soul back together. "To my dying day," she says, "I will keep telling this story."

It's been nine years since this tragedy. The power of forgiveness has not faded.

Endnotes

1. "Forgiveness." Retrieved from www.dictionary.com.
2. "Forgiveness." *Webster's Dictionary.* Thomas Nelson Publishers. © 1991 Nashville, TN.
3. Colossians 3:12,13. Emphasis added. (NKJV).
4. Ephesians 4:32.
5. 2 Corinthians 5:10 (NLT).
6. Matthew 18:22.
7. Philippians 4:13a (Jubilee 2000).

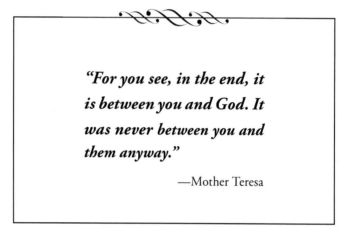

"For you see, in the end, it is between you and God. It was never between you and them anyway."

—Mother Teresa

Chapter Three

Repentance

What It Is and What It Is Not

John the Baptist preached in the Desert of Judea a short and compelling message:

"Repent, for the kingdom of heaven is near."[1]

Immediately following His wilderness temptation, Jesus began to preach:

"Repent, for the kingdom of heaven is near."[2]

There can be no question about it—we are to repent.

Repentance is often a neglected subject as evidenced by Amazon's total of 3,218 books on repentance compared to 12,137 books on forgiveness. As we look at those numbers we see a stark contrast between the two. Could it be that repentance is harder to talk about, write about, and read about because the focus is on you instead of others? As we begin to study repentance, we need to have a good understanding of what it is and what it isn't. Let's first look at some common definitions.

What is Repentance?

Repentance: *a deep sorrow for a past sin.*[3]

Repentance: *personal acknowledgement of a specific wrong.*[4]

Repentance: *Greek "metatonia," is translated as "change your mind and to think differently."*[5]

Repentance: *Hebrew "nacham" is translated as "to turn, to be sorry, and to regret."*[6]

Repentance IS: Defined in scripture as, *"They should repent and TURN to God and PROVE their repentance by their deeds."*[7]

Repentance IS NOT: Just saying, "I'm sorry."

It is clear that God's definition of repentance requires more action on our part, because repentance is so much more than just saying you're sorry; it is showing you're sorry.

CHOOSE2 REPENT

As we begin our "how-to" section on repentance, I would like to direct your attention to my favorite Scripture on this subject:

> *"If we confess our sins (repent) he is faithful and just to forgive us our sins and to cleanse us from all unrighteousness."*[8]

The act of confessing releases out of your mouth an acknowledgement of your sin. Confessing is the trigger that initiates God's response to forgive. Don't miss this important point. You have an active role to play. Make Repentance an intentional action: **CHOOSE2** CONFESS.

This Scripture is the perfect example of what I call the "IF/THEN Principle." Look at what God is saying ... **IF** we do our part, **THEN** He will do His. We are invited to partner with God. And as we see here in 1 John 1:9, the bottom line is, you confess; then He cleans up the mess.

"God's great love for us is demonstrated by
His readiness to forgive us at any moment
— all we have to do is confess."

It is comforting to know that no sin is too great to be forgiven. Scripture teaches us that every sin has been paid for, *"He (Jesus) is the atoning sacrifice for our sins, and not only for ours but also **for the sins of the whole world."**[9]

After all, *"the kindness of God leads you to repentance."*[10]

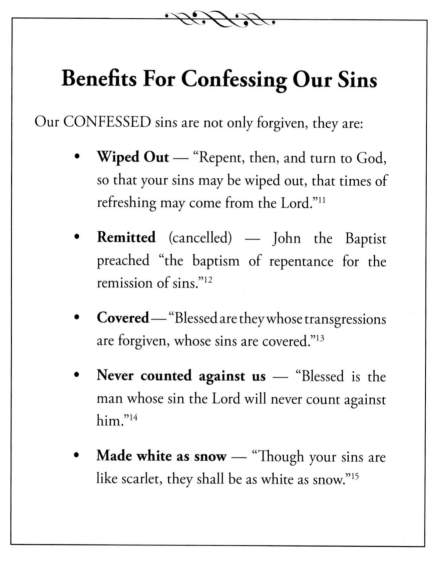

Benefits For Confessing Our Sins

Our CONFESSED sins are not only forgiven, they are:

- **Wiped Out** — "Repent, then, and turn to God, so that your sins may be wiped out, that times of refreshing may come from the Lord."[11]

- **Remitted** (cancelled) — John the Baptist preached "the baptism of repentance for the remission of sins."[12]

- **Covered** — "Blessed are they whose transgressions are forgiven, whose sins are covered."[13]

- **Never counted against us** — "Blessed is the man whose sin the Lord will never count against him."[14]

- **Made white as snow** — "Though your sins are like scarlet, they shall be as white as snow."[15]

"Praise the Lord, O my soul, and forget not all his benefits—who forgives all your sins ..." [16]

A Repentance Worth Emulating

Nobody exemplified Repentance better than King David. In Psalm 51, also known as "The Prayer of David," he repented for his grievous sins against God: the sins of adultery and murder. As David acknowledged his guilt and repented, his burden was released through God's forgiveness, allowing his restoration with God to begin.

> *"Have mercy on me, O God, according to your unfailing love; according to your great compassion blot out my transgressions. Wash away all my iniquity and cleanse me from my sin. For I know my transgressions and my sin is always before me. Against You, You only have I sinned and done what is evil in your sight* (vs. 1) *. . . Cleanse me with hyssop, and I will be clean; wash me, and I will be whiter than snow* (vs. 7) *. . . Create in me a pure heart O God and renew a right spirit within me* (vs. 10) *... Then I will teach transgressors your ways, and sinners will turn back to you"* (vs. 13).

David's prayer demonstrates that REPENTANCE begins with **sorrow** when you RECOGNIZE your mistakes are sin. It's a godly sorrow, a conviction by the Holy Spirit, that draws you toward Him with a heartfelt desire to change.

> *"Godly sorrow brings repentance that leads to salvation and leaves no regret, but worldly sorrow brings death."*[17]

David's life reflected his deep commitment to living a life in "right standing" with God (righteousness). He gave God permission to search the very core of his being, his heart, for any unconfessed sin. *"Search me, O God, and know my heart; test me and know my anxious thoughts. See if there is any offensive way in me, and lead me in the way everlasting."*[18]

"Repentance requires greater intimacy
with God, than with our sin."

God's focus is on the condition of the heart. David's heart was set on obedience to God from his youth. God directed Samuel to go to David's family to find the next king for Israel. The most likely sons were not God's choice, much to Samuel's surprise. God told Samuel, *"The Lord sees not as man sees … but the Lord looks on the heart."*[19] God chose David because of his heart.

"God reads more than our lips; He reads our hearts."

The following testimony about David reveals what God saw in him that Samuel did not, *"I have found David son of Jesse a man after my own heart."*[20] David's heart was humble and his prayer is worth emulating.

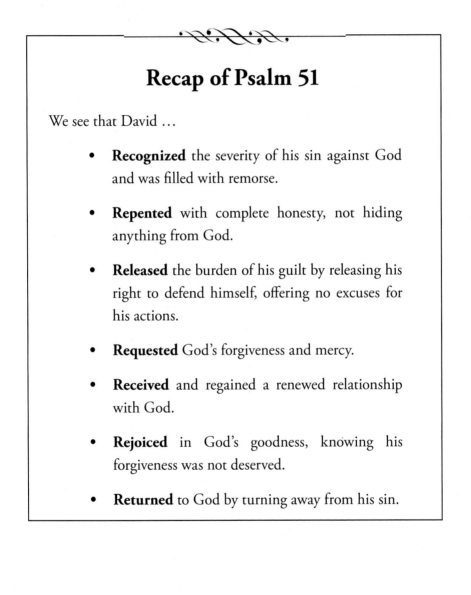

Recap of Psalm 51

We see that David …

- **Recognized** the severity of his sin against God and was filled with remorse.

- **Repented** with complete honesty, not hiding anything from God.

- **Released** the burden of his guilt by releasing his right to defend himself, offering no excuses for his actions.

- **Requested** God's forgiveness and mercy.

- **Received** and regained a renewed relationship with God.

- **Rejoiced** in God's goodness, knowing his forgiveness was not deserved.

- **Returned** to God by turning away from his sin.

This is such a beautiful example watching David co-labor with God. David did his part—he humbly repented, fervently sought God by requesting forgiveness, and turned from his sin. Then, God did His part, fulfilling His promise—He heard David's prayer and forgave his sins. Here's how David put it,

> *"I acknowledged my sin to you, and I did not cover my iniquity; I said, 'I will confess my transgressions to the Lord,' and you forgave the iniquity of my sin."*[21]

> *"The sacrifices of God are a broken spirit, a broken and contrite heart, O God, you will not despise."*[22]

Now let's compare David's humble heart with another heart described in Scripture, *"Whoever conceals his transgressions will not prosper, but he who confesses and forsakes them will obtain mercy. Blessed is the one who fears the Lord always, but whoever hardens his heart will fall into calamity."*[23] When we compare the blessing of mercy that a transparent and humble heart receives, versus the consequences of calamity for the closed and hardened heart, its obvious which one God prefers ... the humble one.

"A humble heart cries out in repentance while the hardened heart arrogantly laughs."

Let me ask you, what is the condition of your heart? Just like with David, God looks upon your heart. Your actions reflect what is rooted in your heart. Luke 3:8a says, *"Produce fruit in keeping with repentance."* "Fruit" is a visible manifestation of its unseen root. You will know when your repentance has taken place ... your behavior (fruit) will change and your relationship with God will be restored.

The Roots of Two Kingdoms

The following pages can help you identify the root from which various characteristics grow. My hope is that this visual illustration will provide the spiritual wake up call (conviction) for you as it did for me eight years ago when I first laid eyes on it. As I examined the fruit of each kingdom, I had to ask myself a hard question, "Which kingdom do I serve?" My conviction was overwhelming. My response, when I was made aware of the "fruit" reflected in my behavior, brought me to my knees in repentance.

Jesus said, *"By their fruit you shall recognize them."*[24]

"... walk in a manner worthy of the Lord, fully pleasing to Him, bearing fruit in every good work ..."[25]

The ROOT from the KINGDOM OF GOD bears GOOD fruit.

When your life is rooted in LOVE (God's Kingdom), it allows the Holy Spirit to produce beautiful, God-honoring fruit in you. The result? Your words, actions, and thoughts reflect His character. Your life is bountiful. The following words describe the "fruit," revealing the Kingdom it's "rooted" in. Ask yourself, **"Am I ... ?"**

Kind	Wise	Obedient
Dependable	Considerate	Honest
Faithful	Merciful	Calm
Stable	Joyful	Loving
Virtuous	Good	Diligent
Fair	Hopeful	Selfless
Pure	Devoted	Gentle
Patient	Disciplined	Courageous
Cooperative	Peaceful	Ethical
Trustworthy	Mature	Teachable
Humble	Truthful	Repentant
Charitable	Edifying	Thankful
Positive	Compassionate	Content
Grateful	Healthy	Understanding
Just	Righteous	Forgiving
Generous	Encouraging	Thoughtful
Cheerful	Gracious	Caring

"This is to my Father's glory, that you bear much fruit, showing yourselves to be my disciples."[25]

The ROOT from the KINGDOM OF DARKNESS bears BAD fruit.

When your life is rooted in BITTERNESS, demonic spirits are able to manifest their "works" through you. The result? Your words, actions, and thoughts are filled with judgment, bitterness, unrest and strife. Your life is a wasteland. Ask yourself, **"Am I ... ?"**

Critical	Bitter	Anxious
Irritated	Annoyed	Afraid
Angry	Greedy	Ashamed
Deceitful	Selfish	Hopeless
Worried	Cruel	Violent
Arrogant	Jealous	Unforgiving
Destructive	Defiant	Confused
Judgmental	Disappointed	Offended
Doubtful	Immoral	Depressed
Revengeful	Unstable	Lustful
Prideful	Abusive	Condemning
Dishonest	Rude	Addicted
Manipulative	Untrustworthy	Negative
Traumatized	Sick	Envious
Rebellious	Covetous	Unsatisfied
Fearful	Disobedient	Hateful
Tormented	Accusing	Spiteful

"Likewise, every good tree bears good fruit,
but a bad tree bears bad fruit."[26]

Is your life ...

Rooted in LOVE   ## Rooted in BITTERNESS

"And I pray that you being rooted ... in LOVE ... may be filled to the measure of all the fullness of God."

Ephesians 3:17, 19

"See to it that ... no root of BITTERNESS springing up causes trouble and thus contaminates many.

Hebrews 12:15 (CJB)

"Choose this day whom you will serve."

Joshua 24:15 ESV

CHOOSE2 EXAMINE YOUR FRUIT

A personal, thorough examination of the "fruit" listed here will help you identify which Kingdom is ruling and reigning in your life. Even though both roots are unseen, their existence does not go unnoticed. Just like Derek Prince said, "You can't see the wind, but you can see what the wind does." The tangible evidence of each kingdom is seen in their fruit. If seeing this chart has convicted you, as it did me, make the healthy choice and **CHOOSE2** PRUNE. *"Either make the tree good and its fruit good, or make the tree bad and its fruit bad; for the tree is known by its fruit."*[27] To help you "prune" you will find a repentance prayer at the end of this chapter.

Excerpt from "The Gift of Forgiveness" by Denise Renner:

"Unforgiveness that isn't dealt with sinks deep down inside a person and becomes a root of bitterness … Like a malignant tree, its evil roots spread out and dig their way deeper and deeper into a person's soul. Every day that an offense is retained and bitterness is allowed to grow and fester on the inside, the clock keeps ticking and those roots just keep going down deeper. Meanwhile, bitterness keeps on producing its terrible harvest of fear, judgmental attitudes, sickness, lack of peace, anger, envy, and jealousy.

But thank God there is a Deliverer, a Forgiver, a Savior whom we can call on to set us free from bitterness and all of its tormentors! I know this from personal experience, because Jesus came to deliver me as I called out to Him day and night.

He went deep into my soul where no human could touch, and pulled out every root and trace of bitterness and unforgiveness that had been growing inside me.

I couldn't be sharing this message of forgiveness with you if that hadn't happened. God wouldn't have been able to trust me. If I had continued to live with the poisonous root of bitterness on the inside of me, I would have been too dangerous for God to entrust me with His precious Body of Christ.

You see, as one called to stand and minister the Word, I have an awesome responsibility. I am accountable to God for what I deliver unto His people. Therefore, I couldn't teach this message of forgiveness **if I had not repented** of my selfish, unforgiving attitude and if Jesus had not delivered me from every remnant of unforgiveness and its horrible companion, bitterness."

A Story of Repentance

"I wish my story was a stand-alone story, but unfortunately mine is one that is all too common. I was educated, had a devoted wife, two children I adored, a nice home, and a good job. My family and I all knew Jesus as Lord and Savior. Not only did I read my Bible, I had studied it for years. You see, I was an ordained pastor. How many times had I read about King David's temptation that led to adultery? Too many to count.

Somehow I thought that could never happen to me. But it did. An attractive woman was hired to be the church secretary. In time, as closeness came from the work environment and the details of her unhappy marriage unfolded, I began a descent down a slippery slope. I knew better, but I engaged in an adulterous affair anyway. This affair came with an enormous price tag. I lost the trust of my wife, my children, and my church. The secretary's price was equally as expensive.

My shame and guilt equaled that of King David. Fortunately, his story held the key for my life, which was now in shambles — repentance. In complete brokenness, offering no defense or excuse for my actions, I repented of my sin to God, to my wife, to my children, and to my church. **My story is one of repentance, but theirs is one of forgiveness.** As they extended forgiveness to me, just as God had done, my family made a commitment to stay with me. I knew my repentance was complete, but my actions over time would provide the evidence that true repentance had taken place.

My church also forgave me, but I am no longer in the pulpit. Every day, as I go to my new job instead, I am reminded of my loss. But every evening as I return to my family, I experience the joy of restoration that forgiveness and repentance brings."

—Pastor *(Identity Protected)*

"You know that you have mastered repentance
when: given the opportunity to repeat
the same sin ... you choose not to."

If you have identified any "fruit" from which you need to repent, pray this prayer:

Heavenly Father, I come to you now and repent for reflecting the bad fruit from the kingdom of darkness in my life. I confess that I have been _____* and ask you to forgive me. I command the demonic spirit of_____* to leave me now. I invite your Holy Spirit create in me a clean heart and renew a right spirit within me. Please give me the strength and courage to make the needed corrections. In Jesus' name I pray, Amen.

*Fill in the blank with a fruit from the chart on page 37 that you want removed from your life.

Endnotes

1. Matthew 3:2.
2. Matthew 4:17.
3. "Repentance." Retrieved from www.dictionary.com.
4. "Repentance." *Webster's Dictionary*. Thomas Nelson Publishers. © 1991 Nashville, TN.
5. *Strong's Concordance*. Entry 3341. Retrieved from http://biblehub.com/greek/3341.htm.
6. *Strong's Concordance*. Entry 5162. Retrieved from http://biblehub.com/hebrew/3341.htm.
7. Acts 26:20b.
8. 1 John 1:9 (ESV).
9. 1 John 2:2 (Emphasis added).
10. Romans 2:4b (NASB).
11. Acts 3:19.
12. Mark 1:4 (KJV).
13. Romans 4:7.
14. Romans 4:8.
15. Isaiah 1:18b.
16. Psalms 103:2.
17. 2 Corinthians 7:10.
18. Psalm 139:23,24.
19. 1 Samuel 16:7 (ESV).
20. Acts 13:22.
21. Psalms 32:5.
22. Psalms 51:17.
23. Proverbs 28:13-14 (ESV).
24. Matthew 7:16a.
25. Colossians 1:10 (ESV).
26. Matthew 7:16a, 17.
27. Matthew 12:33 ESV.

"Repentance is a result of God's kindness, not a prerequisite for it."

Chapter Four

Activation

A Call to Arms and Awareness

<u>A</u>RT: An In-Depth Look at the First Step of the Prayer Model

The A.R.T. prayer model is a 3-step tool. Understanding the purpose and significance of this first step and its scriptural support is crucial as you begin your navigation on the path to personal freedom and transformation.

The "A" step removes your spiritual enemy by:

- the **ACTIVATION** of your **AUTHORITY** in the name of Jesus

- wearing God's **ARMOR** and

- using His **AMMUNITION**.

This warfare step makes the model unique as it confronts the "works" of your spiritual enemy's scheme of unforgiveness that gets initiated when you become offended. Each time you **CHOOSE2** FORGIVE and REPENT, it disrupts and destroys those "works." This was a huge revelation to me as I began to learn about my enemy, that he was an *unseen third party* involved in my anger and resentment, when I held bitterness towards those who had hurt me. I always thought the conflict was just between me and my offender. Scripture proves otherwise.

Unforgiveness is a Demonic Scheme

Let's uncover how enemy attacks against us can be tied to the issue of forgiveness. A primary scheme that Satan uses on his mission to *"steal, kill, and destroy"* is **unforgiveness**. The Apostle Paul spotlights this battle tactic in 2 Corinthians 2:10-11. In speaking to the church at Corinth, he instructed the members to forgive someone who had caused them all grief. Paul chose to forgive this individual and stated the reason why; *"I have **forgiven** in the sight of Christ for your sake, **in order that Satan might not <u>outwit</u> us**. For we are not unaware of his schemes."* Do you want to know how you can avoid being outwitted by Satan's scheme of unforgiveness? Paul gives us the answer—**forgive**.

Unfortunately, I have found that unforgiveness is an active and prolific demonic snare that keeps many believers trapped in bitterness, myself included. If the enemy can hurt you by using other people to upset you with disappointments, unmet needs, or trauma, then a door is opened for his ugly root of bitterness to get planted. For instance, if you are holding a "grudge" towards

Unforgiveness keeps believers trapped in bitterness.

someone or have pain in a memory, this is evidence indicating that you have demonic "works" that need to be destroyed. Grudges grow like weeds once the root gets established. A grudge acts as sludge, clogging your arteries with unforgiveness making you a prime candidate for a spiritual heart attack. Too many believers are in need of bypass surgery not only to survive, but to thrive.

Holding a grudge toward someone also demonstrates that Satan has been successful in another one of his demonic schemes—directing your aim at the wrong "enemy." *"For our struggle is not against flesh and blood, but against the rulers, against the authorities, against the powers of this dark world and against <u>the spiritual forces of evil</u> in the heavenly realms."*[2] Those spiritual forces of evil are the "unseen third party," the real enemy, in the middle of unforgiveness! This is exactly why the prayers incorporate spiritual warfare. All evil spirits must be cast out of any offenses, thereby destroying their "works," which we experience as grudges, resentment, and bitterness, just to name a few. **Without this step to ACTIVATE your AUTHORITY in the Name of Jesus over your enemy by casting him and his "works" out, you have not removed the "unseen third party" of demonic interference from your life.** The "A" step shines the spotlight, illuminating this unseen and uninvited squatter, allowing for his eviction. Truly this step is what sets this prayer apart from all others.

Spiritual Warfare Established

When you become a believer in Jesus, by default you entered a battle zone. It is an invisible battlefield against an unseen enemy, which makes you vulnerable to believe it's not real, but this war is very real. The term, Spiritual Warfare, implies there is a "war" and if there's a war, there must be opposing sides. Here's the conflict:

*"The thief (Satan) comes only to
steal and kill and destroy."*[3]

versus

*"I (Jesus) came that they may have
life, and have it abundantly."*[4]

Satan's goal is to pollute your mind with deception, accusations, temptations, anger, resentment, and bitterness, which renders you ineffective, unable to stand in victory, and receive all the blessings God has designed for you. Jesus initiated and set in motion warfare strategies aimed at the removal of your enemy. When he cast out demons it disrupted their plans, thus destroying their "works." When you do the same, you are set free from enemy captivity and are no longer held as a "prisoner of war." Take back what the enemy stole, the "spoils of war"—peace, joy, health, and freedom—that Jesus purchased for you on the cross. This is how you triumph over the enemy in victory.

*"But thanks be to God! He gives us the
victory through our Lord Jesus Christ."*[5]

Understanding the Battlefield—
The War is Fought in Your Mind

Your battle takes place within your spiritual "command center,"—your mind. King Solomon made a connection between your mind and your heart, *"For as he thinks in his heart, so is he."*[6] When your heart gets broken through an offense, it's very easy for the enemy to affect the way you think. You must learn how to harness the power of your thoughts because this is where the battle can be won or lost. You will learn more about this in Chapter 6 as we examine how the enemy's lies get stuck in your mind and how you can successfully remove them.

As we continue to investigate Spiritual Warfare, I'd like to explain the two pivotal "A" words, **ACTIVATION** and **AUTHORITY**.

Activation

The first step begins with ACTIVATION, which simply means, "to initiate, to start, to set in motion." Your ACTIVATION in this warfare begins by speaking the prayers **ALOUD**. You cannot defeat the enemy with thoughts. You must wage war with words. As you pray aloud, you set in motion or release the power of the words themselves. Proverbs 18:21 teaches the enormous power our words contain, *"The tongue has the power of life and death."* Prayer is to be said, as Jesus instructed, *"He said to them, 'When you **pray, say**: Father, hallowed be your name.'"*[7] Throughout this book, we will be taking our battle instructions directly from Jesus and Do What Jesus Did (DWJD). Therefore, **CHOOSE2** ACTIVATE YOUR MOUTH. Your authority is concealed until you do.

Authority

The definition of AUTHORITY is "the power and/or right to enforce obedience." It is the legal right to use power. We know that words contain power, but when it comes to going up against your spiritual enemy, you also need SPIRITUAL AUTHORITY. Jesus is the only One who has it. Jesus said, *"**All authority** in heaven and on earth has been given to me."*[8]

Scripture also teaches that demons are subject to the power of Christ's authority.

> *"So He traveled throughout Galilee, preaching in*
> *their synagogues and driving out demons."*[9]

> *"The people were all so amazed that they asked each*
> *other, 'What is this? A new teaching—and with authority!*
> *He even gives orders to evil spirits and they obey Him'"*[10]

When you <u>combine</u> in prayer the power of <u>your spoken word</u> with the <u>authority</u> of Jesus in His name, you are positioned for <u>victory</u> over the "works" of the devil.

Your enemy is diligently working to keep you ignorant of the authority you have over him. Your Spiritual Authority is part of your identity and inheritance as a believer in Christ. Don't let the devil keep you in the dark about this.

> *"My people are destroyed from lack of knowledge."*[11]

We have the AUTHORITY of Jesus, Himself, to disarm and remove our enemy. Christ's authority trumps the devil's power. Exercise this authority for it belongs to you and was designed to give you victory over your enemy.

> *"And having disarmed the powers and*
> *authorities, he made a public spectacle of them,*
> *triumphing over them by the cross."*[12]

Jesus Gave His Authority to His Disciples

*"When Jesus had called the Twelve together, **He gave them power and authority to drive out all demons.**"*[13]

The Gospel of Mark records their amazing results:

*"They (disciples) went out and preached that people should repent. They **drove out many demons** and anointed many sick people with oil and healed them."*[14]

Jesus Gave His Authority to the Seventy-Two

These men were not disciples, but simply followers of Jesus.

"After this the Lord appointed seventy-two others and sent them two by two ahead of him to every town and place where he was about to go."[15]

More amazing results were reported:

*"**Lord, even the demons submit to us in Your name.**"*[16]

Jesus Gave His Authority to Us—Those Who Believe

"And God raised us up with Christ and seated us with him in the heavenly realms in Christ Jesus."[17]

Following His crucifixion, Jesus gave His authority to all who would believe in Him.

"I have given you authority to … overcome
all the power of the enemy."[18]

"And these signs will accompany those who believe:
In My name they will drive out demons."[19]

Jesus said He gives His authority to drive out demons to **whoever believes in Him.** This means your spiritual authority was given to you by Christ when you accepted Him as Savior. What great news! You do not have to be subject to torment and oppression from any demon. When you use His authority in His name, you can demand demonic obedience. CHOOSE2 USE YOUR AUTHORITY.

Just like the disciples and others reported, I, too, have amazing results to report using the authority and power in His Name.

The day a young man, identified as a gang member, threatened my daughter's life, I flew into action like a mother bear protecting her cub. I drove to her apartment complex, arriving in record time. Because this offense had my adrenalin pumping so hard, I found myself almost speechless. Literally, all I could do was call upon the name of the Lord because I knew He was the only One who could help me. I walked around her apartment building saying, "Jesus" over and over and over again. No fancy prayers, just that Name. It turns out His Name, was all I needed. After that day, he was never seen again in the complex. This was odd because, he hung out there nightly. Two years later, while shopping at the local mall, she froze when she him saw standing behind the register at her checkout line. He was the cashier. When their eyes met, her fear turned to stunned disbelief, as he greeted her with a big smile and called her by name. He briefly told her his story. She now knows that the day he threatened her he was high, got into more trouble, was arrested and sent to jail. While doing time, a prison ministry team came. Through them he met Jesus. Now he is transformed—drug free, working, and a new creation in Christ.

My advice: Never underestimate the power in the NAME of Jesus.

"Therefore God exalted him to the highest place
and gave him <u>the name that is above every name,</u>
that at the name of Jesus every knee should bow, in
heaven and on earth and under the earth."[20]

Disturbing News

The Barna Group conducted a nationwide survey that reported 40% of Christians do not believe Satan exists.[21] These results are quite surprising, especially since, **"One third of scripture focuses on Satan, most of which comes directly from Jesus.** Demons are mentioned up to 82 times in the Bible (61 times in the Gospels), again mostly by Jesus."[22] I stand on the authoritative word of scripture that Satan is real and not the funny little red devil with horns, a long tail and pitchfork as we so often see him depicted. We can never defeat an enemy whose very existence we deny. Scripture teaches, "Have nothing to do with the fruitless deeds of darkness, but rather **expose them.**"[23]

"Sad to say, the reality of an enemy is the
least taught truth from the pulpit today."

By exposing Satan and his "works," you have two huge advantages over him. First, he will no longer be able to operate in darkness or under the radar—undetected. Secondly, through forgiving, as the Apostle Paul has declared, Satan <u>may not outwit you</u> with his schemes. **CHOOSE2** KNOW YOUR ENEMY, not to exalt him, only to expose him.

Satan is Your Enemy

*"Be self-controlled and alert. **Your enemy the devil** prowls around like a roaring lion, looking for someone to devour."*[24] The word "prowls" is written in the present tense because that is exactly what he is actively doing right now.

He is Not Here Alone

*"… that ancient serpent **called the devil, or Satan**, who leads the whole world astray. He was hurled to the earth, and **his angels (demons) with him**."*[25]

Attributes of Satan (and his Demons)

- **Satan is a Liar**

  *"Not holding to the truth, for there is no truth in him. When he lies, he speaks his native language, for **he is a liar and the father of lies**."*[26]

  His deception prevents you from walking in the truth of who God says you are. In essence, he steals your true identity in Christ—loved, forgiven, and blessed—and gives you a false identity—unforgiven and condemned.

- **Satan is an Accuser**

*"For the **accuser** of our brothers, who accuses them before our God day and night, has been hurled down."*[27]

He uses internal accusations of shame and guilt to make us feel condemned. As a result, you become more vulnerable to thoughts of low self-esteem and worthlessness.

- **Satan is a Tempter**

*"Jesus, full of the Holy Spirit, returned from the Jordan and was led by the Spirit in the desert, where for forty days he was **tempted by the devil**."*[28]

Temptation is a demonic trap. Don't take the bait of Satan by being offended, staying angry, and holding unforgiveness.

- **Demons Have Power**

*"For our struggle is not against flesh and blood, but against the rulers, against the authorities, against the **powers** of this dark world and against the spiritual forces of evil in the heavenly realms."*[29]

However, Jesus has greater power! Satan is a defeated foe. Warfare always exposes the supremacy of Jesus.

*"You, dear children, are from God and have overcome them, because the One who is in you is **greater than** the one who is in the world."*[30]

"The reason the Son of God appeared was to destroy the devil's work."[31]

- **Demons Have Knowledge**

The demon in the man at the synagogue stated: "I know who you are—the Holy One of God."[32]

"Moreover, demons came out of many people, shouting, 'You are the Son of God!'"[33]

Demons knew who Jesus was. Nothing has changed in over 2,000 years. Many people, then and now, are blinded to Christ's true identity, but the demons see clearly.

- **Demons Have Physical Reactions to God**

*"You believe that there is one God. Good! Even the demons believe that—**and shudder**."*[34]

They know who God is and the power He has over them.

- **Demons Have the Ability to Speak**

The demon in the man living in the country of the Gerasenes asked: *"What do you want with me, Jesus, Son of the Most High God?"*[35]

Schemes of Satan (and his Demons)

- ### They Interrupt God's Plans

  *"For we wanted to come to you—certainly I, Paul did, again and again—but **Satan stopped us.**"*[36]

- ### They Lead You Astray

  *"The great dragon was hurled down—that ancient serpent called the devil, or Satan, who **leads the whole world astray.**"*[37]

- ### They Hold You Captive

  *"And that they will come to their senses and escape from the trap of the devil, who has **taken them captive** to do his will."*[38]

- ### They Blind Your Mind

  *"The god of this age has **blinded the minds** of unbelievers, so that they cannot see the light of the gospel of the glory of Christ, who is the image of God."*[39]

- ### They Possess People (Physically)

  *"Then Satan **entered** Judas . . ."*[40]

  *"In fact, as soon as she heard about Him, a woman whose little daughter was **possessed by an evil spirit** came and fell at His feet."*[41]

- **They Oppress People**

  *"And you know that God anointed Jesus of Nazareth with the Holy Spirit and with power. He went about doing good and healing all who were **oppressed** by the devil."*[42]

  Oppression means, "control of or unjust treatment by."[43]

- **They Devour Your Good Work**

  *"And I will rebuke the **devourer** for your sakes, and he shall not destroy the fruits of your ground."*[44]

- **They Imitate or Counterfeit God's Miracles**

  *"But then Pharaoh called the wise men and sorcerers— the magicians of Egypt, and they also did the **same thing** by their occult practices."*[45]

A popular arena where Satan's counterfeiting is displayed is in the occult. Clairvoyants, mediums, fortune tellers, palm readers, tarot cards, horoscopes, and spirit guides are all counterfeits.

- **They Masquerade As Angels Of Light**

  *"And no wonder, **for Satan himself masquerades as an angel of light**. It is not surprising, then, if his servants masquerade as servants of righteousness."*[46]

You will read Karen's story of her encounter with an "angel of light" at the end of this chapter.

Jesus' Warfare Tactics

As we engage in spiritual warfare through the prayers, we are going to emulate Jesus by doing what He did.

- He called the demonic spirits by name.

- He drove demonic spirits out.

- He waged war with The Word.

Jesus Called the Demonic Spirits by Name

- *"Then Jesus asked him, 'What is your name?* **My name is Legion**,' *he replied, for we are many."*[47]

- *"For God has not given us a* **spirit of fear**, *but of power and of love and of a sound mind."*[48]

- *"If the* **spirit of jealousy** *comes upon him ..."*[49]

- *"... And the* **evil spirits** *left them."*[50]

- *"He rebuked the* **unclean spirit!**"[51]

- *"... follow* **deceiving spirits** *and things taught by demons."*[52]

- *"Pride goes before destruction,* **a haughty spirit** *before a fall."*[53]

- *"... And a garment of praise instead of a* **spirit of despair**."[54]

- *"And behold, there was a woman who had a* **spirit of infirmity**."[55]

- *"... That a certain slave girl possessed with a* **spirit of divination**."[56]

In these scriptures, the demon's **name** seems to be descriptive of their function (work) or fruit. In our culture, we often name people by the work they do, for example, doctor, lawyer, or plumber. By naming your enemy based upon their works, for example: **worry**, you can take better aim at the **spirit of fear**. Name your enemy in these prayers because that's exactly what Jesus did. That way there is no question about who you are evicting. The prayer scripts in Chapter 7 will help you do just that. My prayer life was transformed when I realized I had a way to call out a demon by name, based upon its "works" in my life, and that I had the authority, through the name of Jesus, to command them to leave. For more help in identifying the works of your enemy and his name, refer to the fruit chart in Chapter 3. This chart may help you name the enemy that you want removed from you life. In the prayer script, you can insert the name in the blank, making your prayer strategic as you focus your aim. **CHOOSE2** NAME YOUR ENEMY.

Jesus Drove Demonic Spirits Out

- *"When Jesus saw that a crowd was running to the scene, He rebuked (expressed stern disapproval) of the evil spirit: 'You deaf and mute spirit,' He said, '**I command you, come out of him** and never enter him again'"*[57]

- *"Many who were demon possessed were brought to him, and he **drove out the spirits** with a word."*[58]

- *"He also **drove out many demons**, but he would not let the demons speak because they knew who he was."*[59]

- *"Jesus rebuked the demon, and **it came out** of the boy."*[60]

Notice demons <u>always</u> obeyed Jesus' command for them to leave. When you speak to a demon by name in Jesus' authority, you can expect the same results. **CHOOSE2** COMMAND DEMONIC SPIRITS TO LEAVE.

Jesus Waged War With the WORD

Jesus waged war against His adversary, Satan, by **speaking** the word of God. When Satan confronted Him in the wilderness, Jesus took his "stand" and used the only offensive weapon in God's armor to defeat Satan—the *"sword of the Spirit, which is the word of God."*[61] It wasn't the same physical sword Roman soldiers had as part of their battle armor as described in Ephesians 6; this sword is spiritual. It's the same weapon Jesus used, and the same weapon you can use to defeat your enemy ... the infallible word of God. **"For the word of God is living and active and sharper than any two-edged sword."**[62]

This is how He defeated the enemy with the Word:

- *"The devil said to him ... Jesus answered, '**It is written**.'"*[63]

- *"And he said to him ... "Jesus answered, '**It is written**.'"*[64]

- *"'If you are the Son of God,' he said ... Jesus answered, '**It says:** Do not put the Lord your God to the test.'"*[65]

Notice what happened next, *"When the devil had finished all this tempting, **he left him**."*[66] The word of God defeated Satan and he left Jesus alone. Jesus' example shows us that if you stand your ground and **speak** the word of God, Satan and his demons will leave. *"Resist the devil, and he will flee from you."*[67]

There are two other pivotal words in this "A" section: **ARMOR** and **AMMUNITION**. They are necessary pieces of equipment from God's arsenal. Armor assists you as you Confront the enemy and Ammunition enables you to Conquer him.

Stand Protected in God's Armor

ARMOR is defined as, "coverings worn by warriors to protect the body in battle."[68] God has provided defensive armor for you, "to hold an ironclad position against the enemy without taking any serious blows to yourself."[69] *"Therefore, put on the full armor of God, so that when the day of evil comes, you may be able to stand your ground."*[70] The Apostle Paul tells us to "stand" four times in four verses (Ephesians 6:11-14). No matter what, in battle, keep standing, *"And after you have done everything, to stand."*[71] **CHOOSE2** STAND PROTECTED IN GOD'S ARMOR.

Your Weapon for War

The common weapon for a 21st Century warrior is a gun. You, as a spiritual warrior, have been issued a gun as well—it's your mouth. When enemy attacks come, activate your "gun" (open your mouth) and pull the trigger (speak God's word). Our "bullets," as demonstrated by Jesus, are the word of God. He quoted scripture, disarming Satan every time.

When my son-in-law, Matt, returned from combat in Iraq and Afghanistan, he expressed his gratitude to the United States Marine Corps for his intensive weapon training. Because lives depended on a weapon that was prepared to engage the enemy at a moments notice, he had to keep his weapon prepared to fire at all times. Combat experience validated everything his drill instructor taught. An unloaded and unprepared weapon was useless.

Likewise, in your battle, your "gun" needs to be prepared and loaded with **AMMUNITION**, ready to engage the enemy at a moments notice. The best way to have your chamber loaded with "live ammo" is to memorize scripture. Just like Jesus, you are "locked and loaded," ready to pull the trigger and say, "It is written." *"For the word of God is living and active."*[72]

Live Ammo Examples

- BULLET: **It is written,** *"No weapon formed against me will prosper because greater is He that is in me than he that is in the world"* (Isaiah 54:17; 1 John 4:4).

- BULLET: **It is written,** *"I am more than a conqueror in Christ Jesus and at the name of Jesus every knee shall bow"* (Romans 8:37; Philippians 2:10).

- BULLET: **It is written,** *"God has not given me a spirit of fear but of peace, love, and a sound mind. I will be anxious for nothing. His peace fills my heart"* (2 Timothy 1:7; Philippians 4:6-7).

Just like Matt with his weapon training, endless hours of practice on the rifle range transforms a soldier into a sharpshooter. You can become a sharpshooter, too, as you repeatedly shoot truth filled scripture at your enemy.

In it's simplest form, here's your battle strategy:

- **READY, AIM, FIRE.**

Ready, Aim, Fire

READY

CHOOSE2 MEMORIZE SCRIPTURE.

Load it in your chamber.

AIM

CHOOSE2 AIM STRATEGICALLY at your spiritual enemy.

Target him by name for better aim.

FIRE

CHOOSE2 WAGE WAR WITH WORDS.

Pull the trigger and Speak.

"So is my word that goes out from my mouth: It will not return to me empty, but will accomplish what I desire and achieve the purpose for which I sent it."[73]

This is how you ACTIVATE your
AUTHORITY wearing God's ARMOR
and using His AMMUNITION.

The Keys to the Kingdom—Bind and Loose

Two of the most strategic words to be used as "bullets" in spiritual warfare were given to us by Jesus—BIND and LOOSE, known as the keys to the kingdom. Warfare training would not be complete without us examining Jesus' promise to Peter when He gave Peter these keys. Jesus said, *"And I tell you that you are Peter, and on this rock I will build my church, and the gates of Hell will not overcome it. I will give you the keys of the kingdom of heaven; whatever you **bind** on earth will be bound in heaven; and whatever you **loose** on earth will be loosed in heaven."*[74] Wow! What a powerful promise that is. It's as if God is saying, "I've got your back when you use these keys." Jesus spoke these same words once again in Matthew 18:18 as He taught all of His disciples this amazing promise. If Jesus spoke it twice, then these keys must hold significant power.

Keys in the physical realm are obviously important. Without my car key I can't even get into the car, let alone start it. I am rendered powerless without the key. Jesus does not want us to be rendered powerless against our enemy so I had to learn how to use His keys. I was clueless how to interpret the words BIND and LOOSE, let alone use them in my every day vocabulary. Since it sounded Greek to me, I thought, why not investigate the meaning of these two words from the original language. As I searched, I found that studying the Greek did indeed provide more insight as to what Jesus was teaching. I discovered my lack of understanding had somehow been ... lost in translation!

Liberty Savard, in *Shattering Your Strongholds,* does an excellent job of teaching the principle of binding and loosing as she explains the meaning from the original Greek.

Bind

The word **BIND** (Greek, "deo") means to tie, knit, and fasten together. These words infer that the "act of binding" joins things together. However, I have often heard, "I bind you, Satan, in the name of Jesus." So my question became, BIND him to what? As I continued my search in scripture, **I couldn't find one example of Jesus ever binding a demon**. So, if Jesus never bound a demon, why should I? Then my next question was, "What should this BIND Key be used for?" I found the answer in the word of God.

- *"My son, keep your father's commands and do not forsake your mother's teaching. BIND them upon your heart forever: fasten them around your neck."*[75]

- *"Fix these words of mine in your hearts and minds: tie them as symbols on your hands and BIND them on your forehead."*[76]

- *"Let love and faithfulness never leave you; BIND them around your neck, write them on the tablet of your heart."*[77]

CHOOSE2 BIND

Scripture clearly shows that God intends for us to bind ourselves to Him and His truth, making the concept of binding, beautiful. **When you *bind* yourself to the good things of God and *loose* yourself from the bad things of the enemy, you are in alignment with the original Greek definition of these words.** Now I understand why this is such a powerful key. The BIND key is designed for our benefit. Binding yourself to God's word makes you a well-prepared soldier and strengthens you as you STAND.

My advice: **CHOOSE2** BIND your body, soul, spirit, emotions and your future to the good things of God. This is my daily declaration:

> "In the name of the Lord Jesus Christ, and in His authority given to me to bind and loose, I choose to bind my mind to the mind of Christ. I bind my will to the will of God. I bind my mouth to His words of life, and I bind my feet to the path God has planned for me."

Binding myself to God and His word, is a sure-fired way to draw close to Him. When I do so, I have noticed a positive effect on my day.

"Draw near to God, and he will draw near to you."[78]

I especially find it helpful to Bind my attitude to the attitude of Christ as directed in Philippians 2:5, *"Your attitude should be the same as that of Christ Jesus … he humbled himself and became obedient to death, even on the cross."* Humility and obedience are two characteristics I want to develop as I seek to become more like Christ.

I want to encourage you to use your words and align yourself with the purpose that God intended with the word Bind. I have included a chart of my 31 favorite daily declarations that I call the "The Blessings of Binding" at the end of this chapter. My prayer is that you choose to speak them and fortify your day, like a vitamin for your soul.

Loose

The word **LOOSE** (Greek "luo") means to unbind, to release, to break up, to dissolve, and to destroy the grip. The following New Testament examples, assembled by Pastor Rick Renner answered for me what

LOOSE meant in very practical ways. Each bolded word below is a direct translation of "luo":

- **Untying** the thongs of a shoe or sandal—Mark 1:7 and Luke 3:16

- **Unfastening** a donkey—Matthew 21:2

- Loosening or **unraveling** of Lazarus' grave clothes—John 11:44

- **Removing** Paul's chains—Act 22:30

- **Destroying the grip** of the enemy (**disentangling** us from demonic control), holding us in captivity—1 John 3:8

- **Break** the seals and open the scroll—Revelation 5:2

He goes on to teach that 1 John 3:8 could be taken to mean: "*… For this purpose the Son of God was manifested, that He might untie people from all the WORKS of the devil, unraveling Satan's hold on them—until the devil's works in people's lives are utterly destroyed and his hostages set free.*"[79] So, every time Jesus cast out and removed a demon, He was demonstrating the true definition of Loose. We should do the same.

CHOOSE2 LOOSE

There is an example in scripture of Jesus using the word Loose to remove a demonic spirit. "*And, behold, there was a woman which had a spirit of infirmity eighteen years, and was bowed together, and could in no wise lift up herself. And when Jesus saw her, he called her to him, and said unto her, 'Woman, you are loosed from your infirmity.' And he laid his hands on her; and immediately she was made straight, and glorified God.*"[80] In verse

12, the word "loosed" is *apoluo*, which means, "to set free fully and set at liberty."[81] When Jesus "loosed" the spirit of infirmity from her, she was fully set free from the crippling effects of her enemy. We have the authority in the name of Jesus to Loose (untie, unfasten, unravel, and remove demons) thereby destroying and demolishing their "works." As you can see, **the LOOSE key was designed to be used against the enemy to free us from evil bondage**.

My advice: **CHOOSE2** LOOSE your mind and behaviors from the evil things of the enemy. This is my daily declaration:

> "In the name of the Lord Jesus Christ and in His authority given to me to Bind and Loose, I choose to Loose the grip of the enemy from my thinking, my words, and my actions."

The Blessings of Binding

Speak these declarations to fortify your day:

Heavenly Father,

I bind my spirit to the Holy Spirit and my soul to His control.

I bind my mind to the mind of Christ so that His wisdom rules my day.

I bind my lips to declarations of authority in the Name above all names.

I bind my hope to Your promises so my joy is made complete.

I bind my hearing to Your words of truth so that I will not be deceived.

I bind my steps to your path so I will not be led astray.

I bind my choices to Your commandments so I will not stumble and fall.

I bind my character to Your fruit so others will see Christ in me.

I bind my attitude to gratitude so thankfulness will fill my thoughts.

I bind my rebellion to repentance so my relationship with You is restored.

I bind my imagination to Your creativity so my dreams reflect your vision.

I bind my heart to Your heart so that Your love will flow through me.

I bind my hands to work of excellence to advance Your kingdom on earth.

I bind my battles to Your victory, as I am more than a conqueror in Christ.

I bind my burdens to Your yoke and my exhaustion to Your rest.

I bind my salvation to Your cross and my hope to Your empty tomb.

I bind my flesh to obedience and my desires to self-control.

I bind my decisions to Your wisdom and my future to Your plans.

I bind my family to Your protection and our needs to Your provision.

I bind my body to Your healing and my weakness to Your strength.

I bind my sins to Your blood and my fears to Your perfect love.

I bind my awareness to Your presence and my emotions to Your peace.

I bind my abilities to Your anointing and my giftings to Your fruit.

I bind my pride to Your humility and my selfishness to Your sacrifice.

I bind my storms to Your shelter and my security to Your might.

I bind my faith to Your Word and perseverance to my trials.

I bind my trust to Your faithfulness and my failures to Your mercy.

I bind my lack to Your abundance and Your blessings to my home.

I bind my tongue to Your taming and my ears to Your voice.

I bind my reverence to Your majesty and my awe to Your greatness.

I bind my tears to Your comfort and my sorrow to Your joy.

Karen's Personal Encounter with an "Angel of Light"

The following is a personal story from my co-author, Karen, that will shed light on the intricate web of deceit our enemy weaves as he masquerades as an angel of light. Karen's desire is for her experience to be a warning about the dangers of the occult. The root word for occult means "hidden, secret, clandestine" and refers to "any system using knowledge of supernatural powers or practices." Today's "system" utilizes a façade of harmless fun—horoscopes, palm reading, and tarot cards, including a visit to your local psychic—to access supernatural information. In Karen's case, demonic activity was cleverly disguised, leading her to a place she could never have imagined.

"I experienced a huge tragedy back in my 20s when my first husband was killed in a helicopter training exercise with the United States Army. This accident occurred six months after we were married. His sudden death sent my life into a tailspin of inconsolable grief, loss, despair, loneliness, and hopelessness. My prayer over and over and over was just to die. A friend, seeking to give me some hope, told me about a television program that featured a man who had experienced a glimpse into the after-life.

Intrigued, I started to investigate. Before long I learned about a man, Edgar Cayce, and his amazing psychic powers. I was hooked. Reading book after book could not satisfy my desire for answers on the after-life and the unseen spiritual world. Soon books were not enough. I needed (or so I thought) to connect to a real psychic. I was elated believing I had discovered the way I could go on living. All I needed was a good psychic to communicate with my husband, thereby the relationship would not be ended and I would be able to face the next day. So off I went to a spiritualist convention in upstate New York, seeking to find my own personal psychic.

Overhearing a conversation where various psychics were being critiqued, I decided to consult with a woman who was receiving rave reviews. Intent on setting up a future appointment, I set off to locate her within the large convention center complex. I did find her, but that future appointment never happened. As I entered her room, she was finishing a conversation with another individual and began walking over to where I was patiently sitting. As she did so, she raised her hand to her mouth, imitating holding a small radio-like device, and alarmingly cried, "Mayday, mayday. We're going down!" She proceeded to tell me how many men were on the helicopter; that one soldier died on impact, one survived though badly injured, and my husband died on the operating table from extensive injuries. She described him to a "T," including the color of his hair and eyes. She recounted several events from our life together; even describing how he liked to choose a special outfit of mine for each time we went out.

How could she possibly know this much information? I'd never even spoken to her. She didn't know my name, but she sure knew what no other human being could possibly know. My mind was reeling. What in the world just happened? I wanted someone to communicate with my deceased husband, but I didn't expect this.

I had no idea at the time but I had blindly walked into a trap set by my enemy when I first started to look for hope "in all the wrong places." Could I ever have imagined that demons were playing with me as a cat plays with a mouse? Not at all.

I had a childhood friend who had been faithfully praying for me since the accident. She knew of my psychic interests and kept telling me I was dabbling in something wrong but

I wouldn't hear a word of it. Everything the psychic said was correct, so what my friend said didn't matter—what I heard was true; what happened was real. Fortunately my friend was persistent. One day she pulled out her Bible and had me read Deuteronomy 18:9-13, "*When you enter the land the Lord your God is giving you, do not learn to imitate the detestable ways of the nations there. Let no one be found among you who sacrifices his son or daughter in the fire, who practices divination or sorcery, interprets omens, engages in witchcraft, or casts spells, or who is a medium or spiritist or who consults the dead. Anyone who does these things is detestable to the Lord, and because of these detestable practices the Lord your God will drive out those nations before you. You must be blameless before the Lord your God.*"

Those words pierced me, just like a double-edged sword. What I was doing was detestable to God? Oh the grief I felt! I never wanted to do that! For the first time everything became crystal clear. I saw how I was involved in something evil and so much bigger than I could possibly imagine. If God, according to Deuteronomy, forbade these practices, then He could not be the source of anything the psychic told me, no matter how accurate it was. That was impossible. Therefore, if the source was not God, then it had to be demonic because the information came without human knowledge. There was no other option. I was overwhelmed at how much a demon knew about me. With the realization that I was now treading in demon controlled territory, I immediately renounced anything and everything having to do with the occult, repented of my involvement, asked God to forgive me, and dedicated my life to my savior, the Lord Jesus Christ. I have never, not even once, returned to that dark place.

I was an emotionally devastated, vulnerable young woman that my enemy thought he had captured. But through the power of God's love for me, His word did not return to Him void (Isaiah 55:11) but it accomplished His desired purpose—that I should not perish. "For He has rescued us from the dominion of darkness (Satan's kingdom) and brought us into the kingdom of the Son He loves."[82] I have been rescued; I have been set free from my enemy. To God be the glory!"

Perhaps Karen's story resonates with you. If you have had a burning interest in, researched, or participated in any occult activity, the following repentance prayer is provided for you:

"Heavenly Father, I choose to repent from any and all occult practices that I have participated in. I confess _____ (what you did) as sin and I ask you to forgive me. In the name of Jesus, I command the evil spirits of darkness that were assigned to me in this sin to leave me now. Holy Spirit, I invite you to create in me a clean mind with your truth and fill me with your peace."

Endnotes

1. James 3:14,15.
2. Ephesians 6:12.
3. John 10:10a (NASB).
4. John 10:10b (NASB).
5. 1 Corinthians 15:57.
6. Proverbs 23:7 (NKJV).
7. Luke 11:2.
8. Matthew 28:18.
9. Mark 1:39.
10. Mark 1:27.
11. Hosea 4:6
12. Colossians 2:15.
13. Luke 9:1.
14. Mark 6:12-13.
15. Luke 10:1.
16. Luke 10:17.
17. Ephesians 2:6.
18. Luke 10:19a.
19. Mark 16:17.
20. Philippians 2:9.
21. The Barna Group, April 10, 2009.
22. Robert Morris, Free Indeed Audio Series.
23. Ephesians 5:11.
24. 1 Peter 5:8.
25. Revelation 12:9.
26. John 8:44b.
27. Revelation 12:10.
28. Luke 4:1,2.
29. Ephesians 6:12.
30. 1 John 4:4.
31. 1 John 3:8.
32. Luke 4:33.
33. Luke 4:41.
34. James 2:19.
35. Mark 5:7.

36.   1 Thessalonians 2:18.

37.   Revelation 12:9.

38.   2 Timothy 2:26.

39.   2 Corinthians 4:4.

40.   Luke 22:3a.

41.   Mark 7:25.

42.   Acts 10:38 (NLT).

43.   Dictionary.com.

44.   Malachi 3:11a.

45.   Exodus 7:11 (HCSB).

46.   2 Corinthians 11:14.

47.   Mark 5:9.

48.   2 Timothy 1:7 (NKJV).

49.   Numbers 5:14 (NKJV).

50.   Acts 19:12b.

51.   Mark 9:25b (NKJV).

52.   1 Timothy 4:1.

53.   Proverbs 16:18.

54.   Isaiah 61:3.

55.   Luke 13:12 (KJ2000).

56.   Acts 16:16 (NKJV).

57.   Mark 9:25.

58.   Matthew 8:16.

59.   Mark 1:34.

60.   Matthew 17:18.

61.   Ephesians 6:17.

62.   Hebrews 4:12a (NASB).

63.   Luke 4:3,4.

64.   Luke 4:6,8.

65.   Luke 4:9b,12.

66.   Luke 4:13.

67.   James 4:7.

68.   Dictionary.com.

69.   Rick Renner, *Dressed To Kill,* page 356.

70.   Ephesians 6:13a.

71.   Ephesians 6:13b.

72. Hebrews 4:12a.

73. Isaiah 55:11.

74. Matthew 16: 18,19.

75. Proverbs 6:20-21.

76. Deuteronomy 11:18.

77. Proverbs 3:3.

78. James 4:8a ESV.

79. Rick Renner. *Sparkling Gems from the Greek,* page 85.

80. Luke 13:11-13 (NKJV).

81. Ron Phillips. *Everyone's Guide to Demons and Spiritual Warfare,* page 24.

82. Colossians 1:13.

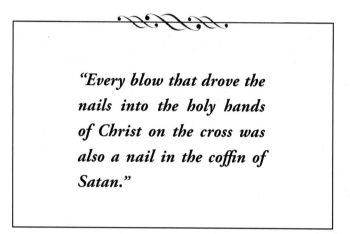

"Every blow that drove the nails into the holy hands of Christ on the cross was also a nail in the coffin of Satan."

Chapter Five

Restoration

A Call to Release

A**R**T: An In-Depth Look at the Second Step of the Prayer Model

Our God is a God of Restoration. He proved it by sending His only Son, Jesus, to be sacrificed on the cross for us. Jesus' blood provided the way to restore our relationship with God that had been broken through sin back in the Garden of Eden. Jesus paid the highest price that could ever be paid for Restoration ... He paid for it with his blood. There can be no doubt about it ... **RESTORATION** is the WILL of GOD.

"And the God of all grace ... will Himself restore you and make you strong, firm, and steadfast."[1]

This chapter will explain in detail the "R" step. "R" stands for **RESTORATION** that you **REQUEST** and **RECEIVE** from the Holy Spirit as you **RELEASE** the debts of others by forgiving. Restoration is "the action of returning something a former owner, place, or condition, or "to renew."[2] That is exactly what this second step of the prayer model initiates.

> *"Create in me a clean heart, O God, and*
> *renew a right spirit within me."*[3]

The Restoration Step in our prayer model is where the REQUEST is made for the Holy Spirit's presence to come and take up residence in the space where the enemy was just evicted. He is invited to restore the areas of brokenness in your life (your heart and your relationships), and to heal the damages from bitterness caused by offenses. As you RECEIVE His presence by faith, He brings His peace, which totally destroys the demonic "works" of strife, stress and worry that were meant to destroy you.

> *"And the peace of God, which **passeth** all*
> *understanding, shall keep your hearts and*
> *your minds through Christ Jesus."*[4]

This explanation of the Greek translation for "**passeth**"[5] denotes that this is a superior peace held high above all other types of peace. In other words, it *excels, surpasses, rises above, is greater than, goes beyond and is over the top* of any other kind of peace that we could seek. I am convinced that requesting and receiving God's peace was key to my personal healing, both physically and emotionally. God's peace is truly supernatural and totally beyond my human understanding. It was able to bring healing to my body that no medication ever could. God's peace really does RESTORE.

"The Spirit of the Lord God is upon me, because the Lord has anointed me to bring good news to the poor. He has sent me to <u>heal the brokenhearted</u> and proclaim liberty to the captives and freedom to the prisoners."[6]

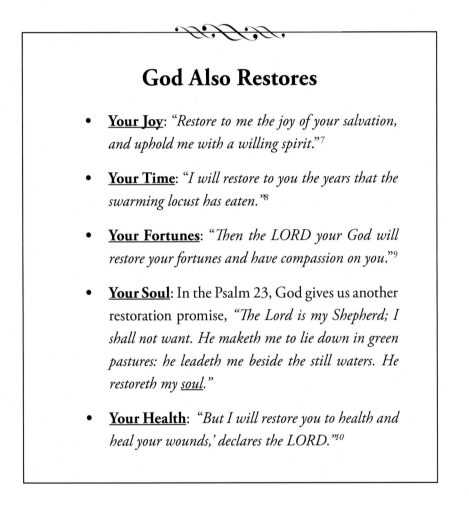

God Also Restores

- **<u>Your Joy</u>**: *"Restore to me the joy of your salvation, and uphold me with a willing spirit."*[7]

- **<u>Your Time</u>**: *"I will restore to you the years that the swarming locust has eaten."*[8]

- **<u>Your Fortunes</u>**: *"Then the LORD your God will restore your fortunes and have compassion on you."*[9]

- **<u>Your Soul</u>**: In the Psalm 23, God gives us another restoration promise, *"The Lord is my Shepherd; I shall not want. He maketh me to lie down in green pastures: he leadeth me beside the still waters. He restoreth my <u>soul</u>."*

- **<u>Your Health</u>**: *"But I will restore you to health and heal your wounds,' declares the LORD."*[10]

CHOOSE2 REQUEST

REQUEST is "to formally ask for something." When you invite (request) the Holy Spirit to be actively involved and to bring His restoration, He will generously respond. This is my favorite scripture to use in my prayer sessions as people are seeking God's will for their lives.

> *"If any of you lacks wisdom, <u>he should ask God</u>,*
> *who gives generously to all without finding*
> *fault, and <u>it will be given to him</u>."*[11]

God invites us to **request** and **receive**. He wants you to bring all of your requests, desires and needs to Him. The following scriptures show just how much God encourages us to ASK.

- *"<u>Ask</u> and it will be given to you; For everyone who asks receives; he who seeks finds; and to him who knocks, the door will be opened."*[12]

- *"You do not have, because you do not ask God."*[13]

- *"This is the confidence we have in approaching God: that if <u>we ask</u> anything according to His will* (and we know Restoration is His will), *He <u>hears</u> us. And if we know that He hears us—whatever we ask—we know that we <u>have</u> what we asked of Him."*[14]

- *"Do not be anxious about anything, but in everything, by prayer and supplication, with thanksgiving, <u>present your requests</u> to God."*[15]

I want you to have confidence that God not only encourages you to request and receive, but that He HEARS you and ANSWERS you as well. Allow the truth of God's word to soak into your heart, as you read the following verses. Knowing that God hears your requests will enable you to go *"boldly before the throne of grace"*[16] with expectation and assurance.

- *"The Lord will <u>hear</u> when I call to Him."*[17]

- *"God has surely <u>listened</u> and <u>heard</u> my voice in prayer."*[18]*"*

- *"Call out to me and I will <u>answer</u> you."*[19]

- *"He will call upon Me, and I will <u>answer</u> him."*[20]

- *"Then you will call, and the Lord will <u>answer</u>; you will cry for help, and he will say: Here am I."*[21]

CHOOSE2 RECEIVE
(The Holy Spirit's Restoration)

The next step is to RECEIVE (to accept) what you requested.

"Therefore, I tell you, whatever you ask for in prayer, <u>believe</u> that you have <u>received</u> it, and <u>it will be yours</u>."[22]

"But when he asks, he must <u>believe and not doubt</u>."[23]

These scriptures show the foundational connection God makes between believing and receiving. The biblical way to know you have received from Him is to believe it by faith. Scripture also states:

"Now faith is <u>being sure</u> of what we hope for and <u>certain</u> of what we do not see."[24]

"And without <u>faith</u> it is impossible to please God, because anyone who comes to him <u>must believe</u> that he exists and that he rewards those who earnestly seek him."[25]

Scripture teaches us that it only takes a small amount of faith to make some big changes. Jesus said, *"I tell you the truth, if you have faith as small as a mustard seed ... Nothing will be impossible for you."*[26]

In the case of RESTORATION, have faith and believe that God CAN restore whatever is broken in your life: your **heart**, your **mind**, your **body**, your **soul**, your **spirit**, your **family**, your **friends**, your **hopes,** your **dreams**, your **future**, your **marriage,** your **strength**, your **joy**, your **purpose**, your **bank account**, your **reputation**, your **confidence**, your **identity**, your **peace,** your **freedom** and your **relationship** with Him and with others. AMEN!

Don't let your faith in God's ability to Restore
be downgraded by your current reality.

"Give us this day our daily bread, and forgive
us our debts as we forgive our debtors."

Release the Debt

Release: "to set free, to let go, to cancel a debt."[27] **When you CHOOSE2 forgive another's debt, you are releasing their obligation to you.** When you are hurt, offended, disappointed, accused, embarrassed, abandoned, blind-sided, traumatized, victimized, or wronged by the actions of others, it feels natural to "expect" an acknowledgement of the wrong they committed. They've incurred a "debt" to you, the least of which is an apology. Too often the "debt" you feel is "owed" to you, does not come. **CHOOSE2** RELEASE their debt anyway. Rip it up, like an "IOU," then you can RIP (rest in peace).

Learning how to forgive by releasing and canceling all debts, saved my marriage. I had a horrible temper. My usual reaction to being disappointed or blind-sided by my husband was extreme anger, which made my mouth a magnet for unkind words, and just like a volcano, it would erupt, spewing words of "death." Instead of releasing, I was keeping *"a record of wrongs"*[28] and expected him to "pay" for each and every one of them. **In effect, his list of offenses became his "debt" to me.** What I did not realize was that holding onto his debt invited the enemy to plant multiple bitter roots in my heart, which grew like weeds and choked out my love for him. To make matters worse, I chose to cover it all up with a smiley face believing the lies that said, "I'm okay," "I'm strong," "I can handle this," and "I don't need help." Believing those lies was like fertilizing my bitter roots with Miracle Grow. I learned the hard way (as my medical records revealed), that NOT RELEASING his debts did not serve me well nor was it God's will for my life.

> *"For man's anger does not bring about the*
> *righteous life that God desires."*[29]

When I began to <u>RELEASE</u> the debts that I felt he "owed" me by forgiving each and every one of them, God's <u>RESTORATION</u> of my health and my marriage began. I was able to see my husband through the eyes of Christ, rather than through the eyes of Rose. My mouth became a magnet for words of "life" which brought restoration to the relationship. Releasing not only changed my life, I can guarantee you, it changed his as well.

"A happy marriage is the union of two good forgivers."

Robert Quillen

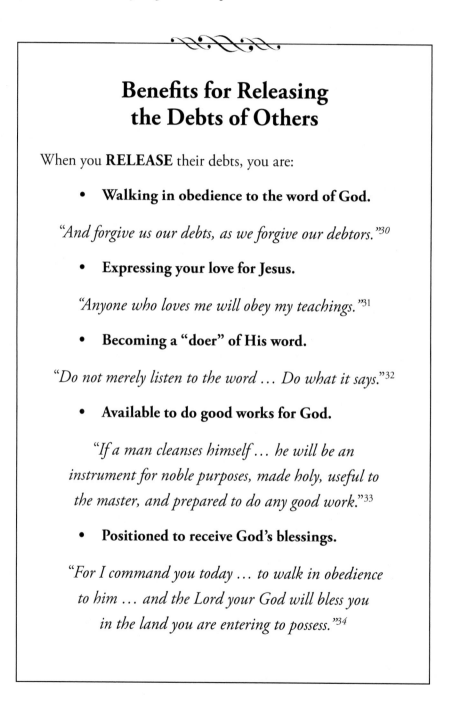

Benefits for Releasing the Debts of Others

When you **RELEASE** their debts, you are:

- **Walking in obedience to the word of God.**

"And forgive us our debts, as we forgive our debtors."[30]

- **Expressing your love for Jesus.**

"Anyone who loves me will obey my teachings."[31]

- **Becoming a "doer" of His word.**

"Do not merely listen to the word ... Do what it says."[32]

- **Available to do good works for God.**

"If a man cleanses himself ... he will be an instrument for noble purposes, made holy, useful to the master, and prepared to do any good work."[33]

- **Positioned to receive God's blessings.**

"For I command you today ... to walk in obedience to him ... and the Lord your God will bless you in the land you are entering to possess."[34]

Release the Debt <u>and</u> The Debtor

As you begin to release, let me encourage you to make your release **complete.** There are two parts to the act of releasing and both are needed to achieve the full potential of "letting go." COMPLETE RELEASE requires:

1. <u>Releasing the debts</u> (offenses) of the person who hurt you AND your need for an apology. In other words, <u>releasing the judgment.</u>

2. <u>Releasing the debtor</u> (offender) to God and allowing God to be the judge and jury, not you. By doing this, you are actually <u>releasing your right to judge.</u>

Complete release is amazing. I can best describe what its like with this word picture. When you forgive both the offense and the offender, it feels like you are shaking off a heavy coat from a hanger that was in your closet. Letting the weight of that coat (which symbolizes the offense) fall to the ground is freeing. The ultimate freedom comes when you are able to drop the hanger (which represents the person) to the ground as well. This leaves your hands empty and totally free to be raised in surrender and praise to the Lord, the One who has the right to judge.

"Will not the Judge of all the earth do right?"[35]

Stories of Restoration

As I recall these true stories to share from my years as a prayer coach, I literally have tears of joy streaming down my face. **I am reminded of just how supernatural God is from these stories of humanly unexplainable transformations.** I am so thankful for the immense privilege it has been to witness HIS restorations first hand, from a front row seat in my office as I've led others through these prayers. It was hard to choose only three testimonies because I can honestly say that God has been faithful to restore each and every time! My prayer is that you, too, will have your own story of restoration reflecting the goodness of God and His power to set the captives free.

"He has sent me to proclaim liberty to the captives and recovering of sight to the blind, to set at liberty those who are oppressed,"[36]

Mark's Story—Restored Relationship

Let me introduce you to Mark, an angry man in his late 50s, living in extreme emotional pain over a broken relationship with his daughter, Becky. Mark's marriage ended in divorce when his daughter was twelve years old, primarily because of his addiction to alcohol. His employment was unstable and so were their finances. His ex-wife, filled with bitterness, could say nothing good about him. Becky was repeatedly told her father abandoned her because he didn't love her. Because she never heard from her dad, Becky believed the lies. What she didn't know was that Mark sent letters and gifts, all of which were returned to him, unopened. He telephoned frequently, but his calls went unanswered. To make matters worse, his in-laws threatened extreme bodily harm if he even came near Becky. What was so frightening, was they had the means to follow through on their threat.

Mark's life began to spiral out of control as he began to believe those same lies. He thought a man like him didn't deserve to have a relationship with his daughter. Finally he stopped trying to contact Becky. Mark was offered a new job, moved away, and many years passed. The twelve-year-old girl was now a young woman in her thirties.

One Sunday afternoon, as I shared with Mark how this 3-step Prayer of Forgiveness had helped me release anger, he agreed to try and forgive his ex-wife for how she destroyed all hopes of a relationship with Becky. Even though this was very hard for him, he chose to take the antidote for hatred —forgiveness for his ex-wife. We could never have anticipated the outrageous blessing God had in store.

> *Mark agreed to try and forgive ...*

Later that very same week, Mark received a message on his phone. It was from Becky. She had attended church with a friend the previous Sunday (the very day he forgave her mother) and had a strong prompting to reach out and find him. Mark could not believe what he was hearing, and with some trepidation, he returned her call. Then he heard the words coming from the other end of the phone ... "Hello, Dad." I have never heard a man sob the way Mark did the day he told me this story.

Mark's re-connection with Becky was sudden and nothing short of a miracle. We don't know how it happened, just that it did. Their restored relationship took time, as they both stayed committed to removing the layers of unforgiveness one by one. Mark and Becky are now experiencing life together as father and daughter, believing that God has restored the years they lost. Becky is free from hate now that she knows the truth—her father always loved her. Mark is free from shame, guilt, self-bitterness, and most amazingly, regret. How the Holy Spirit did this still astounds Mark today.

> *"Now to him who is able to do immeasurably more than all we ask or imagine, according to his power that is at work within us, to him be glory in the church and in Christ Jesus throughout all generations, for ever and ever! Amen."[37]*

Carolyn's Story—Restored Health

Let me introduce you to Carolyn, a 37 year old, beautiful young woman in extreme physical pain. As she entered my office, she struggled to walk on her own and grimaced as she carefully lowered herself into the chair. I asked her, "Carolyn between 1 to 10, with ten being the worst pain you've ever been in, what is your pain level today?" She replied, "I'm at an 8."

Three years earlier, Carolyn was a passenger in a car that had been hit head on, when her friend Sue, the driver, fell asleep at the wheel. Since the accident, Carolyn had endured four surgeries attempting to repair her pelvic injuries and was taking numerous prescription medications for the pain. Even with taking the full dosages, she still found herself in unbearable discomfort. In addition to the physical pain, her husband filed for divorce, citing "stress" as his reason. That day, at a pain level of 8, she was at the end of her rope. Having exhausted every means to get help, her mother called me and made an appointment for prayer.

When I read Ephesians 6:12 to her, *"For our struggle is not against flesh and blood, but against the rulers, against the authorities, against the powers of this dark world and against the spiritual forces of evil in the heavenly realms,"* everything changed. You see, she was entangled in three separate lawsuits as a result of her accident and injuries. She was in a constant battle of getting even. The moment she realized her battle was not against flesh and blood, but against an enemy dedicated to taking her out, she rose to the challenge to destroy his works. Within the 60 minutes we shared together, Carolyn forgave: Sue for falling asleep, the ambulance driver for dropping her as he removed her from the wreckage, her doctor for not taking her seriously when she complained of continuing pain. Repeatedly, as she forgave, the supernatural God of the Universe showed up, releasing a river of peace over Carolyn like I'd never seen before.

As she forgave, God showed up, releasing a river of peace.

When our time was up she hopped out of the chair, grabbed her purse and started for the door to leave. I could not believe my eyes at how she moved so effortlessly. I asked her, "Carolyn, on a scale of 1 to 10, with 10 being the worst pain you've ever been in, what is your pain level now?" She stopped dead in her tracks, turned around and looked at me in shock as she realized she had no pain. As she stood there, frozen for a moment in time, her tears of joy said it all. Sometimes, God's goodness just leaves you speechless.

Mary's Story—Restored Identity

Mary's story is about the person who is hardest to forgive: *yourself.*

Mary is a 45-year-old, devoted wife, role model, and Christian "Volunteer of the Year" at a local food bank. She works full-time as Director of Children's Ministries at her church. She keeps an exhausting schedule and yet cannot sleep at night, which was not only taking its toll on her body, it also presented problems in her marriage. The strategies from marriage counseling weren't providing the relief she needed, so Mary called me for prayer. She was convinced all would be well if I could just help her to forgive her husband. **Shortly into our session, God revealed there was someone else Mary had to forgive—herself.**

As Mary began the repentance process for holding unforgiveness toward her husband, we discovered an impenetrable wall around her heart, hiding a deep secret. Mary lived in self-condemnation for something she did 25 years before. Each time she prayed to forgive her husband, part of her wall of defense started to crumble. It was like she was peeling off, one by one, the spiny, leaves of an artichoke that serve as protection for it's tender heart. The real problem, buried in Mary's heart, was being exposed.

Reluctantly, Mary revealed her deep secret. At age 20, she had an abortion. To her, this sin was so grievous, she could never be forgiven by anyone—not by God, her family—and definitely not by herself. Even though Mary knew God's word promised forgiveness for all repented sin, she did not believe He could forgive her. Instead of being called "Forgiven" by God, Mary's guilt and shame called her "Unforgivable." The enemy, in her case, had masterminded a huge identify theft.

Hidden behind a façade of busyness, Mary was trapped, seeking some kind of absolution by doing good works and people-pleasing. The horrible memories of that day plagued her mind as they incessantly replayed. Nightly, her sleep was interrupted with recurring dreams and unsettled feelings of doom. Her self-loathing graduated to self-punishment. At the age of 27, she decided to have her tubes tied, denying herself the opportunity of ever being a mother. When she married Tony, three years later, she concealed the truth. She told him there would be no children because she was unable to conceive. When her transparency exposed that she needed to forgive herself and not just her husband, I said, "Mary, God has already forgiven you. He's just waiting for you to forgive yourself. May I lead you in a prayer of repentance for your abortion, asking God to forgive you?" Mary shook her head and said, "No, I can't." So I offered to speak on her behalf and lead her through the prayer. I said, "Let's join hands and unite our hearts in agreement that until you can speak, I will stand in the gap for you." This time she nodded in agreement.

Before we prayed, I read her 1 John 1:9, *"If we confess our sins, He is faithful and just and will forgive us our sins and purify us from all unrighteousness."* I then asked her, "Do you believe God's Word is true?" She said, "Yes, I do." God honors the power of agreement in prayer, so I spoke this prayer on her behalf:

"Heavenly Father, in the name of Jesus, I come to You now, filled with remorse for the sin I committed when I aborted my child. I am deeply consumed with grief over this decision and I repent for my actions. Please forgive me and wash me clean from this sin. In the name of Jesus, I command the evil spirits of guilt and shame that are tormenting me to leave me now. I come out of agreement with the accusing spirits that lie to me with thoughts of self-bitterness, self-judgment, self-condemnation, and self-hatred. I command these thoughts to be loosed from my mind. I choose to bind my mind to the mind of Christ and receive His truth about my identity. I am forgiven and with God's help, I choose to forgive myself. Heal my heart, Lord, from the brokenness caused by this trauma. Create in me a clean heart towards myself and remove the pain from the sights, sounds, and smells in these memories. Restore my relationship with You and fill me with Your peace. I will take time now to listen for Your truth and I ask You to set me free."

She nodded in agreement with each word I spoke on her behalf, and we sat there in silence, pausing to listen for God's truth. As tears began streaming down her face, Mary opened her eyes, and announced to me, "God said, 'I love you, Mary.'" Mary was transformed by the renewing of her mind as she transplanted that truth over all of the lies. Jesus came to set the captives free. That's exactly what He did for Mary that day. God restored Mary's sleep, her marriage, and her identity.

"So if the Son sets you free, you will be free indeed."[38]

The two steps you just read about in the previous two chapters (A and R) are inspired from a warning Jesus gave us in Matthew 12: 43-45. It's IMPERATIVE you understand their significance and why they are put together in the prayer model.

> *"When an evil spirit comes out of a man, it goes through arid places seeking rest and does not find it. Then it says, 'I will return to the house I left.' When it arrives, it finds the house <u>unoccupied</u>, swept clean and put in order. Then it goes and takes with it seven other spirits more wicked than itself, and they go in and live there. And the final condition of that man is worse than the first."*

In Step 1, you **Activate** your **Authority** in the name of Jesus to CAST OUT, REMOVE, or DRIVE OUT the evil spirit, leaving your "house" unoccupied and empty.

In Step 2, you <u>must</u> **Request** and **Receive** the Holy Spirit to occupy the space that is now vacant. Therefore, when an evil spirit seeks to return to oppress you, it will find "no vacancy" because you have filled your "house" with the Holy Spirit.

Bottom line—you don't want your final condition worse than before so don't leave the house unoccupied. Immediately fill it with the Holy Spirit.

Endnotes

1. 1 Peter 5:10.
2. Dictionary.com.
3. Psalm 51:10 (ESV).
4. Philippians 4:7 (KJV).

5.   Rick Renner, *Sparkling Gems From the Greek.*

6.   Isaiah 61:1 (HCSB).

7.   Psalm 51:12 (ESV).

8.   Joel 2:25 (ESV).

9.   Deuteronomy 30:3.

10.   Jeremiah 30:17.

11.   James 1:5.

12.   Matthew 7:7,8.

13.   James 4:2b.

14.   1 John 5:14,15.

15.   Philippians 4:6.

16.   Hebrews 4:16.

17.   Psalm 4:3b.

18.   Psalms 66:19.

19.   Jeremiah 33:3a.

20.   Psalms 91:15.

21.   Isaiah 58:9.

22.   Mark 11:24.

23.   James 1:6.

24.   Hebrews 11:1.

25.   Hebrews 11:6.

26.   Matthew 17: 20.

27.   Dictionary.com.

28.   1 Corinthians 13:5.

29.   James 1:20.

30.   Matthew 6:12.

31.   John 14:23a.

32.   James 1:22.

33.   2 Timothy 2:21.

34.   Deuteronomy 30:16.

35.   Genesis 18:25.

36.   Luke 4:18.

37.   Ephesians 3:20,21.

38.   John 8:36.

*C*hapter *S*ix

Transformation

A Call to Transplant

AR**T**: An In-Depth Look at the Third Step of the Prayer Model

This last step encourages you to TAKE the TIME at the end of the prayer to listen for God's TRUTH, then TRANSPLANT His truth into your THINKING. The result is **TRANSFORMATION.**

"Do not conform any longer to the pattern of this world, but be <u>transformed</u> by the <u>renewing of your mind</u>."[1]

This chapter explains how to renew your mind. As you **CHOOSE2** PRACTICE THE ACTION STEPS of "Taking Time" and "Transplanting Truth," you can have your own "after" story of transformation.

At the end of the prayer, I encourage you to be quiet for a moment and wait patiently for God to reveal His divine perspective and give His fresh revelation about your situation. **Intentionally taking the time to be still and listen for God to speak His truth is imperative if you want to be set free from lies that have gone unchallenged in your thinking.** During this time of silence many people have been able to see their situation with increased clarity, similar to a light bulb being turned on in a dark room. God's truth always brings light into your situation, that's why you must take time for it.

> *"But when he, the Spirit of truth, comes,*
> *he will guide you into all truth."*[2]

Transformation Redefined

Before discussing the actions you will be taking in this step, we need to establish a clear understanding of transformation and how it is achieved. Transformation is defined as "a thorough or dramatic change."[3] Often, when people hear the word transformation, they assume it means the same thing as change. Even though they are similar in definition, I have found an acute difference.

- Change is external and reversible. Transformation is internal and permanent.

- Change can be instantaneous. Transformation takes time.

- Change requires an intentional decision to create it and maintain it. Transformation does not. It isn't something you do, it is just what you are.

Your hairstyle, for example, can be changed with a haircut from your hair stylist. To keep it changed, you have to be intentional by scheduling your next appointment or reverse the change by allowing your hair to grow back in. Either way it requires effort on your part.

"A changed mind doesn't stay changed by itself any more than your hair stays combed."

In the case of forgiveness & repentance, **CHOOSE2** BE TRANSFORMED from **OFFENDABLE** to **UNOFFENDABLE**.

You want a supernatural reconstruction of your thinking towards others and you want it to be permanent! Similar to the metamorphosis of a caterpillar into a butterfly (new creation), your transformation takes time to develop. Through the A.R.T. prayer process of forgiving each person and each offense, one at a time, little by little, you are able to emerge from the cocoon of unforgiveness. This is a personal metamorphosis worth striving for.

A butterfly is a transformation, not an improved caterpillar.

"Therefore, if anyone is in Christ, he is a new creation. The old has passed away; behold, the new has come."[4]

CHOOSE2 TAKE TIME

In this action, you ask the Holy Spirit to speak His truth about the person and specific memory, then TAKE the TIME to be still, and wait for His answer. The scriptures below tell us how to prepare to hear from God.

"Be still before the Lord and wait patiently for him."[5]

"For God alone, O my soul, wait in silence."[6]

Being still and waiting in silence invites the
voice of the Good Shepherd to speak.

CHOOSE2 LISTEN

Prior to this step in your prayer, you have been doing all the talking. Now it's God's turn. All too often our prayers only present requests to God, never leaving time for Him to speak. This Listening step is so crucial because it provides the opportunity to receive a key piece of information (TRUTH) that you will transplant into your thinking to dispel the enemy's lies.

*" ... listen to me, and pay attention
to the words of my mouth."*[7]

"My sheep listen to my voice."[8]

I love the way the "Skitguys," in one of their performances, encourage our prayers to be a two-way street of talking and listening. "There is a God, who sent His Son to die on a cross so that He could have a relationship with you. The greatest relationships are the ones where people talk to each other. He longs for you to spend time together with Him and **talk to Him and listen to Him** so that He can be your God, and you can be everything He created you to be."[9]

CHOOSE2 HEAR GOD SPEAK

Being able to hear from God as He specifically "speaks" to you may seem impossible, but I assure you it is not. God "speaks" to us all the time, but you may just be unaware of how He does. By faith, wait expectantly to receive God's truth as He individualizes His answer just for you.

"Give ear and come to me; <u>hear me</u>,
that your soul may live."[10]

Over the years from many prayer sessions, I've learned that God can speak without actually talking. "Hearing" from Him isn't necessarily an audible sound as much as it is a "knowing," a *"still small voice"*[11] or an impression, fresh thoughts and new understanding. *"Be still and <u>KNOW</u> that I am God."*[12]

My favorite way of witnessing God communicate is when He supernaturally removes emotional pain and replaces it with His peace. When His peace fills the room; you can tangibly feel His presence. **God never fails to respond to an invitation to be present in your time of pain.** The power of His amazing peace is impossible to fully convey in words. It passes all understanding.

How Others Heard From God

- Feeling release of a burden, like a weight being lifted

- Being able to take a deep breath, feeling a tension released

- A restful feeling as evidenced by numerous yawns

- Fears reduced and removed as phobias disappear

- Physical pain reduced and often removed

- An inspired, judgment-free understanding of their situation

- Fresh revelation or new thoughts appear

- "Seeing" a mental picture or vision

- "Seeing" colors and lights

- Memories of other people come to mind

- A remembrance of scripture

- Clear thinking instead of confusion

- A stillness over a storm of emotions

- A deep reassurance over worry

- A bubbling up of joy

- An emergence of hope

- Amazing attitude adjustments

I also hear them say, "I am free" and "It is well with my soul." Give God permission to speak to you any time, any day, and any way He chooses. Keep expecting that He will.

A Word of Encouragement

At the end of your time of silence, if you feel that you haven't heard from God, don't be discouraged. This doesn't mean God isn't talking to you. **Listening is a skill that often needs time to be developed.** Keep exercising your listening muscle by providing quiet time with God.

I love what Pastor Chris Hodges from Church of the Highlands in Birmingham, Alabama has to say about this: "When you ask God, 'Why aren't you talking to me?' God replies, 'I already did. It's in My Word.'" Pastor's advice for people concerned about hearing from God is this: "Stop listening for a voice; start looking for a verse."

Don't ever give up on your quest for truth. God speaks through His Word, the Bible. It is a "live" source of contact with Him. *"For the word of God is living and active."*[13]

CHOOSE2 JOURNAL— Your "Pearls" of Wisdom

Many people, myself included, have found it helpful to record in a journal what God revealed to them during their time of silence. I call these "pearls of wisdom." His truth, in each specific situation, is valuable information and vital to <u>record</u> so that you can <u>remember</u> what to <u>replace</u> over the lies from the enemy. Write your "pearls" in a journal so you may refer to them frequently. "String them together" as a reminder that you have embraced forgiveness. My favorite reminder of forgiveness is a pearl bracelet I wear almost daily. It helps keep me accountable to the decision I made to embrace forgiveness as a lifestyle, what I call "forgivin' livin'."

Pearls also represent my favorite example of transformation. It amazes me how God takes the "irritant" from a worthless piece of sand enclosed in the oyster's shell, and transforms it over time into a valuable reflection of beauty. It reminds me of how God causes all things, even irritants, to work together for good (Romans 8:28).

Just like the pearl, you too can be divinely developed into a new creation. **Only your creative God can take the irritant of an offense against you and transform it, through forgiveness, into a beautiful reflection of Him.** You become the *"pearl of great price*[14]*"* and a valuable asset to the Kingdom of God! When you walk in forgiveness, God's **love** is reflected to the world. Like a magnet, others will be drawn to Him when they witness your forgiveness Transformation! **CHOOSE2** BE A PEARL and REFLECT GODS LOVE. It shows the family resemblance to your Heavenly Father, when you allow His love to shine through you.

CHOOSE2 RECOGNIZE THE LIES

Lies are the thoughts that are opposed to what God says in His Word. They are like unseen "land mines" strategically buried by the enemy on the battlefield of your mind. The enemy uses deceptions full of accusations to trip you up as you move toward your divine assignment. The enemy knows that God has good plans for your life, so he will do everything in his power to prevent you from reaching your destiny. He achieves this when you get mentally stuck or hung up on thoughts full of pain from your past instead of looking forward with thoughts full of hope.

"'For I know the plans I have for you,' declares the Lord, 'plans to prosper you and not to harm you, plans to give you hope and a future.'"[15]

All too often when you get hurt by a "land mine" called DISAPPOINTMENT (which is actually a trauma to your heart, soul, and mind), the devil seizes the opportunity to plant LIES in your mind. It's as if with each trauma of disappointment, whether large or small, a real estate OPEN HOUSE sign gets posted, inviting them to "come on in" and dump lies. For instance, disappointments like:

1. **A bad medical report.**

    - This invites the **"voice from the god of all lies"** to say: "You're not going to make it."

    - But the "**Voice from the God of All Truth**" says: *"Do not be anxious about anything, but in every situation, by prayer and petition, with thanksgiving, present your requests to God. And the peace of God, which transcends all understanding, will guard your hearts and your minds in Christ Jesus."*[16]

2. Being overlooked for a promotion; unable to find a job.

- This invites the **"voice from the god of all lies"** to say:"You're so stupid. You're a loser."

- But the **"Voice from the God of All Truth"** says: *"For I can do everything through Christ, who gives me strength,"*[17] and *"My God will meet all your needs according to His glorious riches in Christ Jesus."*[18]

3. The end of a meaningful relationship.

- This invites the **"voice from the god of all lies"** to say: "Nobody cares about you. You'll always be alone. You're worthless."

- But the **"Voice from the God of All Truth"** says: *"And surely I am with you always, to the very end of the age,"*[19] and *"Trust in the Lord with all your heart, and lean not on your own understanding; In all your ways acknowledge Him, and He shall direct your paths."*[20]

Lies downgrade your dreams, while
truth upgrades your faith.

The best way to recognize a lie is to be intimately familiar with the truth. My advice, read God's Word and become familiar with His promises. That way, just like a bank teller, you will be able to immediately recognize a counterfeit (lie). Tellers spend endless hours handling and counting authentic currency as their training to spot a fake and take it out of circulation. **You too, can become keenly aware of counterfeits as you increase your exposure to the truth of God.** The next step will show you how to take the lies out of circulation.

CHOOSE2 TRANSPLANT THE TRUTH

Your transformation depends on your mind being renewed with truth.

Transplanting God's truth into your thinking is the "how-to" process that begins the renewal of your mind. It's the great exchange of God's truth over the enemy's lies.

"Then you will know the truth, and
the truth will set you free."[21]

"Teach me your way, O Lord, that I
may walk in your truth."[22]

Transplanting infers digging up something old and replacing it with something new. Like in the case of a heart transplant, once you discover your old heart isn't working well, removal is scheduled so that a new one can be transplanted into the same place. **Just like the old heart, your toxic thoughts that are not working well must be removed, creating space for God's life-giving thoughts to be transplanted in their place.** This is how you take the old thoughts (counterfeits) out of circulation—you dig them up and replace them.

Transplanting truth in your mind is especially important if you have been believing lies about your true identity in Christ. The enemy loves to create an "identity crisis" in believers with lies about who we are in order to render us ineffective. Don't let enemy accusations influence your belief about who you are, thus creating a negative self-image and devaluing your sense of worth and significance. <u>Don't be deceived into believing that what you did is who you are.</u> Instead, dig up those lies and transplant the following I AM's into your mind and mouth.

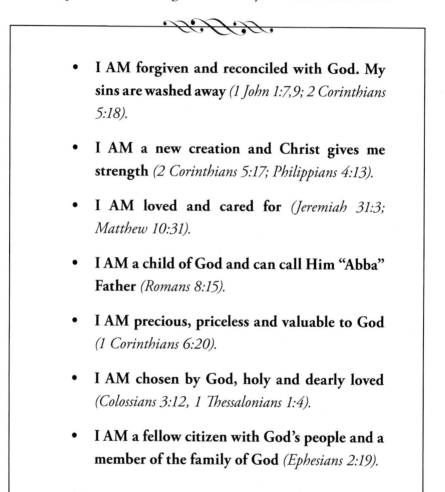

- **I AM forgiven and reconciled with God. My sins are washed away** *(1 John 1:7,9; 2 Corinthians 5:18).*

- **I AM a new creation and Christ gives me strength** *(2 Corinthians 5:17; Philippians 4:13).*

- **I AM loved and cared for** *(Jeremiah 31:3; Matthew 10:31).*

- **I AM a child of God and can call Him "Abba" Father** *(Romans 8:15).*

- **I AM precious, priceless and valuable to God** *(1 Corinthians 6:20).*

- **I AM chosen by God, holy and dearly loved** *(Colossians 3:12, 1 Thessalonians 1:4).*

- **I AM a fellow citizen with God's people and a member of the family of God** *(Ephesians 2:19).*

Transplanting truth prevents identity theft. You'll know your transplanting is successful when you can say every day:

"I AM who the Great I AM says I AM."

Preventative Maintenance

Prevention is key to maintaining good physical health. It is the same for your spiritual health as well. It is better to prevent a root of bitterness from developing into a stronghold thinking pattern than to perform a life-saving transplant. Strongholds are like deep "ruts" on a footpath that develop over time. Your wrong thinking patterns get developed the same way. Over time when lies and judgment-filled thoughts of accusations go unchallenged they get buried deep inside the familiar footpath where the enemy has walked all over you! Do everything you can to prevent lies from taking root in your mind. Here's how:

CHOOSE2 HOLD THOUGHTS CAPTIVE

2 Corinthians 10:5 provides the best prevention advice to keep your thinking patterns healthy. You are to "*take every thought captive*" or put it on hold, before it has a chance to land in your mind in the first place. Then scripture teaches what to do with that thought on HOLD. If it is identified as a LIE, then we are told to DEMOLISH it.

> *"We demolish arguments and every pretention*
> *(lies) that sets itself up against the knowledge*
> *of God (truth), and we take captive every*
> *thought to make it obedient to Christ."*[23]

Think of it this way: your mind is a busy runway where planes filled with thoughts are attempting to land. You are the air traffic controller whose job is to identify and clear planes for landing. When you identify a plane filled with "life giving" God thoughts of faith, hope, love, peace, kindness and forgiveness, **CHOOSE2** give it a GREEN LIGHT, permitting it to land.

> *"Finally, brothers, whatever is true, whatever*
> *is noble, whatever is right, whatever*
> *is pure, whatever is lovely, whatever is*
> *admirable—if anything is excellent or*
> *praiseworthy—<u>think</u> about such things."*[24]

When you identify a plane from your enemy, hoping to land and unload his cargo full of LIES and other garbage: fear, doubt, anger, judgment, condemnation, retaliation, and resentment, CHOOSE2 give it a RED LIGHT, denying landing privileges. Then go one step further, and verbally declare to the enemy: "This runway is closed."

Sift your thought life thoroughly. Filter out any
thoughts you don't want to show up on your tongue.

CHOOSE2 EXTINGUISH ANGER

Another prevention method to stop the enemy from finding a place in your mind is found in Ephesians 4:26 and 27.

> *"In your anger do not sin: Do not let the*
> *sun go down while you are still angry,*
> *and do not give the devil a foothold."*

Don't react in anger. The moment you retaliate with unkind words, react violently, or plot revenge, you've taken the enemy's bait. Instead resolve your anger before the day is over. How? By forgiving. **Forgiveness extinguishes the destructive fire that was set ablaze when you got mad.** Staying angry is the perfect set-up for the devil to initiate his transformation power, for you see, not all transformation is good.

Unresolved anger transformed me from a 21-year-old, starry-eyed bride, hopelessly in love, walking down the aisle to marry my high school sweetheart, into a 51-year-old, bitter spouse, physically ill, headed down the aisle of a courtroom for divorce. Choose carefully what you allow to transform your life. Don't choose anger; it only invites the destruction of your relationships and of your health. **CHOOSE2** RESOLVE ANGER, NOT REACT TO IT. My advice, the moment you feel angry, invite God into your battle and say this prayer:

"In the name of Jesus I command the evil spirit of anger to leave me now. I will not accept the tormentors of rage, hate, and revenge to work in me or through me. Instead, I choose to forgive _____ and ask You, Holy Spirit, to extinguish this destructive fire of anger by filling me with Your peace. Amen."

The Power of the Testimony

When I want to purchase something, especially a big ticket item like a car, I look at the reviews given by people who have gone before me. Their "thumbs up or down" testimonials, based upon firsthand experience, have power to influence my decision. Scripture confirms that a testimony actually does have tremendous power.

"And they have conquered him (the devil) by the blood
of the Lamb and by the <u>word of their testimony</u>."[25]

God has shown me over the years, as I have witnessed many BEFORE and AFTER testimonies emerge, **there is no hurt too deep for Him to heal and no heart too broken for Him to repair.** I have selected segments from actual thank you notes I've received from people who have embraced the A.R.T. of Forgiveness & Repentance. Their words may have the power to influence you to give the A.R.T. model a test drive.

Stories of Transformation

- "The forgiveness prayers restored our marriage. The deep level of forgiveness we achieved now allows my husband and I to be free to put into practice everything we learned from the many marriage counselors we've been going to over the years. It sure would have saved us a lot of time and money if we had known about these prayers first."

- "I can see clearly now. It's like I am looking at my in-laws through a new set of lenses. I was blind, but now I'm free."

- "My 'stinkin' thinkin' about myself is gone. God's grace IS bigger than my mistakes."

- "My life has gone from a 'chaos of crisis' to a relaxed state of 'hardly a care in the world.' I had no idea I was so uptight.'"

- "The prayer scripts you provided are being used so often, I went to Staples and got the sheet laminated so I'll never lose them."

- "These prayers have actually had a neutralizing effect on my fears now that I choose to hold fearful thoughts captive."

- "My post-traumatic stress is gone and I no longer have horrible nightmares."

- **"The choking feeling in my throat every time I swallowed is gone" (sent from a rape victim who was almost strangled to death).**

- "Thank you again for leading me through these prayers. I wanted to let you know that my normal panic attacks have disappeared. I didn't need to be pre-medicated for anxiety going into the tunnel for my latest MRI. I got on the table completely calm."

- "I feel so much lighter. These prayers are like a weight loss program."

- "I never in a million years thought I could ever forgive my Dad, but I did. I feel alive again, like the years have been redeemed."

- "I feel like my heart just got exfoliated as if layers of dead skin were removed."

- "Tonight was the first time I was able to sleep in a dark room" (from a woman with an intense fear of snakes). The thank you note from her husband included… "those prayers got her out of the guest room and back into the bedroom with me."

- "Please consider writing a book about what happened to me. I hope the world gets to read all about the pain-reducing POWER in forgiveness." Her wish came true. Her name is Carolyn; you met her in Chapter Five.

The last testimonial I have included is the story about a young woman's journey to lose an incredible 150 pounds after she discovered she had been believing some lies. This story was reported in the Bluffton Today Newspaper, April 26, 2015. It confirms that …

TRANSPLANTING TRUTH over LIES … TRANSFORMS LIVES.

To make it easier for you to identify the lies this young woman believed, I have **bolded** them in this adaptation from the original article, "It's Been a Journey."

Mother-Daughter Duo Loses Combined 250 Pounds

At 25, Annie Emison weighed 287 pounds at her heaviest. But after a weight-loss journey, she has lost more than 150 pounds and inspired her mother to do the same.

The weight gain started when she moved to Los Angeles for college at 18 years old. Her busy schedule and the adjustment to life away from her family often led her to eat fast food and junk food. And, as she reported to me *no meal was complete without dessert.* "It was way more of a sugar addiction for me," she said. "Food was a party. *Food was the one thing that made me happy.*"

Within a short four months, she had gained about 50 pounds. "The pounds just piled on so quickly," Emison said. "You've heard of the freshman 15—for me it was like the freshman 50." Before she knew it, she was shopping in the plus-size sections at stores, could no longer wear high heels and hid behind baggy clothing. Meanwhile, Emison continued succeeding in a stressful and busy career working with a celebrity hairstylist. Though her life revolved around making others beautiful, she felt the opposite about herself. "I hated myself. I hated the way I looked and I hated the way I felt," Emison said.

By the time she and her husband moved to Bluffton two years ago, Emison had come to believe **she would always be overweight**. After some prayer, she felt led to read Galatians 5:22-23, *"But the fruit of the spirit is love, joy, peace, patience, kindness, goodness, faithfulness, gentleness, and self-control."*

I thought, "God, I have all these things but *I don't have self control —I will always just be fat. You didn't give me control over the food issue in my life*," Emison said. "That's when I realized I was calling God a liar." She prayed for God's help to find the self-control she needed to begin her weight-loss journey.

Emison's mother had struggled with her own weight issues most of her life. So when Emison began her diet and turned down her mother's home-cooked meals, it initially hurt her feelings. "I felt abandoned. I had lost my eating buddy, my Starbucks buddy. I watched her disappear inch by inch and I couldn't believe it—she was being transformed," her mother said.

In January 2014, about six months into Emison's weight loss, her mother decided to make a change in her own life.

"Watching her drop size after size and choosing to love herself was the inspiration for me to start loving myself too," her mother said.

She turned to "No Matter What," her favorite song performed by popular contemporary Christian artist, Kerrie Roberts for inspiration. Originally written as a song declaring love to Jesus, the lyrics were, "No matter what, I'm gonna love <u>you</u>," but she changed the words to, "No matter what, I'm gonna love <u>me</u>." She recalled, "I would stand on the scale every day, look at the numbers and sing those lyrics as my daily declaration. As I walked past the refrigerator, I would do the same. It became my daily pledge of allegiance to choose to love myself."

If you change your mind, you can change your life.

She has lost 100 pounds and Emison has lost 150.

The mother-daughter team has advice for others who might be struggling with their weight and self-image. "'If you change your mind, you can change your life," Emison said.

They also credit God for helping them stay strong and realize new truth and how to love themselves. "It's been a journey of releasing self-hatred and lies," her mother said.

Emison's mother is in the final stages of publishing a book on forgiveness called *The A.R.T. of Forgiveness & Repentance*. In the book, she coaches others with a three-step prayer model and is passionate about encouraging people to choose to **transplant truth over lies.**

Yes, you read that right. This is my story too. Annie Emison is my daughter.

Annie and Rose

Before & After

Endnotes

1. Romans 12:2a.
2. John 16:13.
3. Dictionary.com.
4. 2 Corinthians 5:17.
5. Psalms 37:7a (ESV).
6. Psalms 62:5a (ESV).
7. Proverbs 5:7.
8. John 10:27a.
9. Skitguys.com, Psalm 139.
10. Isaiah 55:3a.
11. 1 Kings 19:13 (KJV).
12. Psalms 46:10a.
13. Hebrews 4:12a.
14. Matthew 13:46 (KJV).
15. Jeremiah 29:11.
16. Philippians 4:6,7 (NLT).
17. Philippians 4:13 (NLT).
18. Philippians 4:19
19. Matthew 28:20
20. Proverbs 3:5,6 (NKJV).
21. John 8:32.
22. Psalms 86:11a.
23. 2 Corinthians 10:5.
24. Philippians 4:8.
25. Revelation 12:11 (ESV).

Chapter Seven

The Tool of Transformation

The Forgiveness & Repentance Prayers

Drum roll please … the moment has arrived! It's time to present the 3-step prayer model and explain why these two prayers have been intentionally linked together.

**The intention of the Forgiveness Prayer is for you to:
set your "debtors" FREE from "owing" you anything.**

&

**The intention of the Repentance Prayer is for you to:
be set FREE from the "debt" you owe God.**

This is the "ultimate" in personal freedom;
what I call "FREE indeed."

The Forgiveness Prayer

When you **CHOOSE2**FORGIVE, you are cooperating with God's will and being obedient to the Lord's Prayer in Matthew 6:12: *"Forgive our debts as we forgive our debtors."* **Declare your intent by saying:**

"Heavenly Father, I bind my will to your will as I choose to forgive _____(who)_____ for _____(what they did)_____ .
I forgive _____(who)_____ and cancel his/her debt.
He/she owes me nothing, not even an apology."

Activate your Authority

A   "In the name of Jesus, I **ACTIVATE** my authority and command the demonic spirits of __ bitterness, anger, and resentment ___ to leave me now."

Request Restoration

R   "Holy Spirit, I request that you come and fill the places where the enemy has been removed. I invite you to heal my heart and remove the pain from this memory. Create in me a clean heart toward _____(who)_____ and renew a right spirit within me. **RESTORE** my body, mind, and soul with your peace."

Transplant Truth

T   "I invite you, Holy Spirit, to transform my thoughts with your **TRUTH**. I take time now to be still and listen. Tell me your truth that will set me free."

Pause and listen. *Record God's truth. Transplant that truth into your thinking, then continue with the Repentance Prayer.*

Romans 12:2—*"be transformed by the renewing of your mind."*

The Repentance Prayer

When you **CHOOSE2**REPENT by confessing your sin, God is faithful to forgive you and wash you clean of all unrighteousness (1 John 1:9). **Declare your intent by saying:**

> "Heavenly Father, I come to you now and confess that I
> have held bitterness and judgment toward
> ___(who)___. I am sorry and I ask you to forgive me."

Activate your Authority

A "In the name of Jesus, I **ACTIVATE** my authority and command all demonic spirits involved in my unforgiveness toward ____(who)____ to leave me now. I have forgiven (who)___ and release all judgment against them. God has forgiven me for this and now I choose to forgive myself. I command the demonic spirits of ___(shame, guilt, and self-condemnation)___ to leave me now."

Request Restoration

R "Holy Spirit, I request that you come and fill the places where the enemy has been removed. I receive your forgiveness and ask you to wash me clean of all unrighteousness. Please **RESTORE** my body, mind, and soul with your peace."

Transplant Truth

T "Thank you, Father, for forgiving me. I take time now to be still and listen for your **TRUTH** about ME that will transform my mind and set me free."

Pause and listen. *Record God's truth. Transplant*
that truth into your thinking.

John 8:36—*"So if the Son sets you free, you will be free indeed."*

When all three A.R.T. steps are combined, the Forgiveness Prayer is spoken like this:

The Forgiveness Prayer

"Heavenly Father, I bind my will to your will as I choose to forgive ____(who)____ for ____(what they did)____. I forgive ____(who)____ and cancel his/her debt. He/she owes me nothing, not even an apology. In the name of Jesus, I activate my **AUTHORITY** and command the demonic spirits of ____(bitterness, anger, and resentment)____ to leave me now. Holy Spirit, I request that you come and fill the places where the enemy has been removed. I invite you to heal my heart and remove the pain from this memory. Create in me a clean heart toward ____(who)____ and renew a right spirit within me. **RESTORE** my body, mind, and soul with your peace. I invite you, Holy Spirit, to transform my thoughts with your **TRUTH**. I take time now to be still and listen. Tell me your truth that will set me free."

When all three A.R.T. steps are combined, the Repentance Prayer is spoken like this:

The Repentance Prayer

"Heavenly Father, I come to you now and confess that I have held bitterness and judgment toward __(who)__. I am sorry and I ask you to forgive me. In the name of Jesus, I **ACTIVATE** my authority and command all demonic spirits involved in my unforgiveness toward __(who)__ to leave me now. I have forgiven __(who)__ and release all judgment against them. God has forgiven me for this and now I choose to forgive myself. I command the demonic spirits of __(shame, guilt, and self-condemnation)__ to leave me now. Holy Spirit, I request that you come and fill the places where the enemy has been removed. I receive your forgiveness and ask you to wash me clean of all unrighteousness. Please **RESTORE** my body, mind, and soul with your peace. Thank you, Father, for forgiving me. I take time now to be still and listen for your **TRUTH** about ME that will transform my mind and set me free."

The scripts provide space for you to personalize each prayer, as you enter the name of the person ___(who)___ and their offense ___(what they did)___. Personalizing the prayers this way allows you to peel back the layers of memories, one at a time, just like peeling an onion. The other blank provided is for the name of the enemy you want to remove from this memory. The example I gave in the Forgiveness Prayer included the most common enemies of ___(bitterness, anger, and resentment)___. You can use those or personalize your warfare by naming an enemy you have identified (See Chapter 3 Fruit Chart). Even though an offense has come through a person, your battle is not against flesh and blood. The prayers enable you to forgive the person and kick out your real enemy at the same time.

Now I would like to share with you an exercise that has helped many people get the personalization process started. These next pages are designed to help you identify the people (debtor) and their offense against you (debt).

Digging Up Debts Exercise

Search your heart as I ask you these questions. Fill in the blanks with your honest answers.

- Are you angry? At whom _____

    Why_____

- Are you holding a grudge? Against whom _____

    Why_____

- Are you annoyed with anyone? Who_____

  Why_____

- Are you offended by anyone? Who_____

  Why_____

- Are you irritated by anyone? Who_____

  Why_____

- Are you holding a judgment against anyone? Who_____

  Why_____

- Are you not speaking to anyone? Who_____

  Why_____

- Are you gossiping about anyone? Who_____

  Why_____

- Are you accusing anyone? Who_____

  Why_____

- Are you keeping a record of wrongs toward anyone? Who_____

  Why_____

Has anyone ever?   **Who**   **How**

Disappointed you   _____   _____

Blind-sided you   _____   _____

Embarrassed you   _____   _____

Insulted you   _____   _____

Humiliated you   _____   _____

Bullied you   _____   _____

Abandoned you   _____   _____

Betrayed you   _____   _____

Neglected you   _____   _____

Rejected you   _____   _____

Deceived you   _____   _____

Condemned you   _____   _____

Falsely accused you   _____   _____

Assaulted you   _____   _____

Violated you   _____   _____

Cursed you   _____   _____

Cheated on you   _____   _____

Lied to you   _____   _____

Broken your heart   _____   _____

Physically abused you   _____   _____

Verbally abused you   _____   _____

Has anyone robbed you of your?	Who	How
Peace	_____	_____
Trust	_____	_____
Joy	_____	_____
Dreams	_____	_____
Security	_____	_____
Future	_____	_____
Belongings	_____	_____
Confidence	_____	_____
Reputation	_____	_____
Purity	_____	_____
Desire to live	_____	_____
Safety	_____	_____
Hope	_____	_____
Strength	_____	_____
Ideas	_____	_____
Plans	_____	_____
Needs	_____	_____
Health	_____	_____
Friends	_____	_____
Family	_____	_____

Each time a client agrees to participate in this exercise, they **CHOOSE2** DIG UP DEBTS. This indicates their hunger to be set free. When they return for prayer with names and offenses written on these pages, I'm not only humbled for the opportunity to lead them through the prayers, I am ecstatic because I know God will set them free. You will be too. So, may I say to you, if you took the time to fill this out, I am proud of you and want to pray this blessing over you.

"May the Lord bless you and give you the courage to conquer every single issue brought up in this exercise. May the Lord bless you in your obedience to forgive each and every one. May the Lord bless you and cause His face to shine upon you and give you His peace." Amen.

CHOOSE2 MAINTAIN YOUR FREEDOM

Pray often. Repeat the Forgiveness & Repentance Prayers as often as needed until the bitterness towards another person is gone. Wounds, especially caused by trauma, are very deep and often require repeated prayer to remove the many layers that have accumulated over the years. The more you **CHOOSE2** EMBRACE the A.R.T. model, the more liberated you become. I had to repeat the prayers often to finally be set free. I still embrace this model daily, because in the case of forgiveness, the old saying, "practice makes perfect" is so very true.

"Forgiveness is like faith; you have to keep reviving it."

Mason Cooley

Pray quickly. Like a "knee-jerk" reaction, the moment you feel offended, hurt, or angry, immediately make the healthy choice to forgive. Do not let the sun go down on your anger! Do yourself a huge favor and forgive quickly before bitterness sets in. This will save you a lot of unnecessary damage from the stress caused by an offense.

"Forgiveness is not an occasional act,
it is a constant attitude."

Martin Luther King Jr.

Pray in defense. Keep standing against the enemy because freedom gained is not the end of spiritual warfare. Pastor Ron Phillips teaches, "It is only the beginning of a life of discipleship. Ground retaken in one's life must be defended. Sin must be purged and a life of commitment continued. We must wear our armor until that day we exchange it for a robe of white."[3] Be vigilant to protect your heart and mind. Proverbs 4:23 admonishes us to, *"Above all else, guard your heart (mind) for everything you do flows from it."*

Guard your heart and mind with the fierceness of
a watchdog. Prevent entry to any accusing thought,
like an intruder intent on a home invasion.

Power in Your Testimony

Use the power of your forgiveness testimony when the enemy tries to reignite the flames of anger toward someone you already forgave. When that happens, **CHOOSE2** SPEAK YOUR TESTIMONY to overcome the enemy by saying:

"I have forgiven_____ and they owe me nothing, not even an apology. In the name of Jesus, I command the accusing spirit to leave me now. Come Holy Spirit and restore my mind and body with your peace. Amen."

CHOOSE2 SPEAK A BLESSING

To cement the deal of forgiving someone, speak a blessing over them.

"Do not repay evil with evil, or insult with insult, but with blessing, because to this you were called so that you may inherit a blessing."[4]

"But I tell you who hear me: Love your enemies, do good to those who hate you, bless those who curse you, pray for those who mistreat you."[5]

The best prayer you can pray for someone is for their salvation.

"You will know that forgiveness has begun when you recall those who hurt you and feel the power to wish them well."

Lewis Smedes

Since the first day I sat down to write this book, my prayer has been that God will use it to inspire and encourage everyone who reads it to begin a personal journey toward freedom as they learn how to forgive and repent.

On this journey together through the past seven chapters, if you have forgiven even one person or offense then this book has indeed served its designated purpose.

I pray you will continue to deliberately align your choices with God's will and accept the challenge to disrupt and destroy the devil's scheme of unforgiveness. I want you to believe that with God's help you can do it and be radically resolved to never quit pursuing this divine challenge.

Forgiveness is the heart of God.
It always was and it always will be.

Embrace the heart of God ... **CHOOSE2** FORGIVE.

Endnotes

1. Matthew 6:14,15.

2. Psalm 139:23,24.

3. Ron Phillips. *Everyone's Guide to Demons and Spiritual Warfare,* page 26.

4. 1 Peter 3:9.

5. Luke 6:27, 28.

6. 2 Timothy 2:21.

Appendix

The Greatest Transformational Prayer of All

I want to introduce you to another prayer of transformation because this one is the greatest transformational prayer of all time. When you invite Jesus to be your Lord and Savior, you are transformed into a new creation from:

UNFORGIVEN to FORGIVEN

Heaven isn't for good people, it's for forgiven people.

Let me ask you a few questions. Have you confessed your sins to God so that your relationship with Him can be restored? Have you received God's promise of forgiveness for your sins? If you haven't already, I'd like to show you how.

1. <u>Recognize</u> your need for reconciliation with God by acknowledging you have sinned: *"For all have sinned and fall short of the glory of God."*[1]

2. <u>Repent</u> of your sins because sin separates us from God: *"But your iniquities have separated you from your God."*[2]

3. <u>Believe</u> in Jesus and His power to save you: *"For God so loved the world that He gave His only Son, that WHOEVER believes in Him shall not perish, but have eternal life."*[3]

4. <u>Receive</u> the Father's love for you: *"Yet to all who received Him, to those who believed in His name, He gave the right to become children of God."*[4]

5. <u>Confess</u> Him as Lord: *"If you confess with your mouth, 'Jesus is Lord,' and believe in your heart that God raised him from the dead, you will be saved."*[5] *"There is no other name under heaven by which man can be saved."*[6]

6. <u>Accept</u> your free gift of salvation: *"For by grace you have been saved, through faith, and that not of yourselves; it is the gift of God."*[7]

"EVERYONE WHO CALLS ON THE NAME OF THE LORD WILL BE SAVED."[14]

This free gift of salvation was best illustrated for me by my second-grade Sunday School teacher. Her story gave me a word picture about salvation being a gift brought to me by Jesus. Miss Mary said, "Just imagine it's your birthday and the doorbell rings. You run, open the door and see Jesus standing there with a beautifully wrapped present for you. Even though the gift has your name on it, it only becomes yours when you reach out and take it. The moment you bring it into your home, and unwrap it, it's yours forever. Jesus stands at the door for every single person and has their gift waiting for them too. Unfortunately, some people don't hear the doorbell ring or ever take the gift out of His hands." Miss Mary encouraged us to take the gift from Jesus.

The Salvation Prayer

This same offer from Jesus is here for you today. He is standing at the door of your heart. You have a choice to make. You can either **CHOOSE2** RECEIVE His free gift of salvation or leave Him standing at the door. It's up to you. Of course, like Miss Mary did for me, I encourage and invite you to open the door to your heart now, reach out and accept His free gift of salvation. If this is your desire, repeat this prayer out loud:

"Dear Jesus, Thank you for dying on the cross for me to wipe away my sins. I confess that I am a sinner who needs a Savior. I repent for my sins and I ask you to forgive me. I believe in my heart that you were raised from the dead and I invite You to come into my life to be my Lord and Savior. I accept Your free gift of salvation." Amen.

WELCOME TO THE FAMILY OF GOD! Heaven is rejoicing over the choice you just made, "*I tell you that in the same way there will be more rejoicing in heaven over one sinner who repents.*"[8] You can be assured of your salvation. Nothing can separate you from the love of God.

If you prayed this prayer we would love to hear from you. Please contact us at **info@embracetheART.org** so we can rejoice together!

*"I write these things to you who believe in
the name of the Son of God so that you may
KNOW YOU HAVE ETERNAL LIFE."*[9]

You may wonder what you should do next. My advice for you is:

1. Get your own Bible and begin reading. Let God instruct you from His written word.

2. Seek out a community of believers (church) to receive much needed encouragement on your walk of faith, *"Let us not give up meeting together ... but let us encourage one another."*[10]

3. Be baptized. *"Repent and be baptized, every one of you, in the name of Jesus Christ for the forgiveness of your sins, and you will receive the gift of the Holy Spirit."*[11]

4. Supplement your training. I have received excellent teaching from many online and television ministries, for example:

   • Dr. Ron Phillips and Dr. Ronnie Phillips, Jr. at
   www.abbashouse.com

   • Pastor Robert Morris at
   www.theblessedlife.com

   • Pastor Chris Hodges at
   www.churchofthehighlands.com

Their extensive archives are readily available to you.

Now, let's celebrate together because we have this promise in Philippians 1:6:

"Be confident of this, He who began a good work in you will carry it on to completion until the day of Christ Jesus."

Endnotes

1. Romans 3:23.
2. Isaiah 59:2.
3. John 3:16.
4. John 1:12.
5. Romans 10:9.
6. Acts 4:12.
7. Ephesians 2:8.
8. Romans 10:13.
9. Luke 15:7a.
10. I John 5:13.
11. Hebrews 10:25.
12. Acts 2:38.

$\mathcal{A}$ppendix

Ministry Resources

Dr. Art Mathias
Wellspring School of Ministry
   2511 Sentry Drive
   Anchorage, AK 99507
   www.akwellspring.com
   907-563-9033

Dr. Ron Phillips; Dr. Ronnie Phillips, Jr.
Abba's House
   5208 Hixson Pike
   Hixson, TN. 37343
   www.abbashouse.com
   423-877-6462

Pastor Robert Morris
Gateway Church
   700 Blessed Way
   South Lake, TX 76092
   www.theblessedlife.com
   888-799-1949

Pastor Chris Hodges
Church of the Highlands
4700 Highlands Way
Birmingham, AL 35210
www.churchofthehighlands.com
205-980-3079

Pastor Rick Renner
Rick Renner Ministries
P.O. Box 702040
Tulsa, OK 74170-2040
www.renner.org
918-496-3213

To learn more or connect with us:

Embrace the A·R·T Ministries

Rose Carlin & Karen Lundblad

198 Okatie Village Dr.

Ste. 103-323

Bluffton, SC 29909

www.embracetheART.org

Visit our website for your FREE downloadable
CHOOSE2 Chart and to schedule
Rose for a speaking engagement.